Becoming a ~~Twenty~~-First Century Church

Clarence Sexton

CROWN CHRISTIAN PUBLICATIONS

Royal Reading

FAITHFORTHEFAMILY.COM

First Edition
Copyright
August 2005

FaithfortheFamily.com

Becoming a First Century Church

Copyright © 2005
Crown Christian Publications
Powell, Tennessee 37849
CrownChristianPublications.com
FaithfortheFamily.com
ISBN: 1-58981-277-8

Layout by Stephen Troell

Printed in the United States of America

Dedication

This book is affectionately dedicated to an innumerable host of whom the world was not worthy, who through the centuries remained faithful to God.

All of us have been influenced greatly by others. After more than thirty-eight years in the ministry, this principle of influence means more to me than ever.

I owe a tremendous debt to many men and women who have influenced my life. My precious wife has been steadfastly supportive through all these years. We "press on" together.

Men such as my first pastor, Dillard Hagan; my "Paul," Lee Roberson; Bible teacher, Frank Sells; and pastor and author, Peter Masters, have provided by their influence much of the thought found in this book.

I thank you, faithful men, for your love and devotion to our Lord and His Word. We must have a revolution back to the Bible. This revolution will bring us face to face with the first century church.

Clarence Sexton
Acts 5:42

Contents

"And the word of the Lord was published throughout all the region." Acts 13:49

INTRODUCTION

APOSTOLIC CHRISTIANITY

C. H. SPURGEON

I shall confine myself to the text. It being an old custom to take texts when we preach, I have taken one, but I shall address you, at large, upon a subject which I am sure will occupy your attention, and has done for many days and years past—the subject of gospel missions.

We feel persuaded that all of you are of one mind in this matter, that it is the absolute duty as well as the eminent privilege of the Church to proclaim the gospel to the world. We do not conceive that God will do His own work without instruments, but that, as He has always employed means in the work of the regeneration of this world, He will still continue to do the same, and that it becomes the Church to do its utmost to spread the truth wherever it can reach the ear of man. We have not two opinions on that point. Some churches may have, but we have not.

Our doctrines, although they are supposed to lead to apathy and sloth, have always proved themselves to be eminently practical; the fathers of the mission were all zealous lovers of the doctrines of the grace of God; and we believe, the great supporters of missionary enterprise, if it is to be successful, must always come from those who hold God's truth firmly and boldly, and yet have fire and zeal with it, and desire to spread it everywhere.

But there is a point on which we have great division of opinion, and that is as to the reason why we have had so little success in our missionary labours. There may be some who say the success has been proportionate to the agency, and that we could not have been more successful. I am far from being of their opinion, and I do not think they themselves would express it on their knees before Almighty God. We have not been successful to the extent we might have expected, certainly not to an apostolic extent, certainly with nothing like the success of Paul or Peter, or even of those men who have preceded us in modern times, and who were able to evangelize whole countries, turning thousands to God.

Now, what is the reason of this? Perhaps we may turn our eyes on high, and think we find that reason in the sovereignty of God, which hath withholden His Spirit, and hath not poured out His grace as aforetime. I shall be prepared to grant all men may say on that point, for I believe in the ordination of everything by Almighty God. I believe in a present God in our defeats as well as in our successes; a God as well in the motionless air as in the careering tempest; a God of ebbs as well as a God of floods. But still we must look at home for the cause. When Zion travails, she brings forth children; when Zion is in earnest, God is in earnest about His work; when Zion is prayerful, God blesses her. We must not, therefore, arbitrarily look for the cause of our failure in the will of God, but we must also see what is the difference between ourselves and the men of apostolic times, and what it is that renders our success so trifling in comparison with the tremendous results of apostolic preaching.

I think I shall be able to show one or two reasons why our holy faith is not so prosperous as it was then. In the first place, we have not apostolic men; in the second place, they do not set about their work in an apostolic style; in the third place, we have not apostolic churches to back them up; and in the fourth place, we have not the apostolic influence of the Holy Ghost in the measure which they had it in ancient times.

First, We Have Few Apostolic Men in These Times

I will not say we have none; here and there we may have one or two, but unhappily their names are never heard; they do not start out before the world, and are not noted as preachers of God's truth. We had a Williams once, a true apostle, who went from island to island, not counting his life dear unto him; but Williams is called to his reward. We had a Knibb, who toiled for his Master with seraphic earnestness, and was not ashamed to call an oppressed slave his brother; but Knibb, too, has entered into his rest. We have one or two still remaining, precious and treasured names; we love them fervently, and our prayers shall ever rise to heaven on their behalf. We always say, in our prayers, "God bless such men as Moffat! God bless those who are earnestly toiling and successfully labouring!"

But cast your eyes around, and where can we find many such men? They are all good men; we find no fault with them; they are better than we; we, ourselves, shrink into nothingness compared with them; but we must still say of them that they are less than their fathers, they differ from the mighty apostles in many respects, which we think even they would not be slow to own. I am not speaking of missionaries only, but of ministers too; for I take it we have as much to mourn over in regard to the spread of the gospel in England as in foreign lands, and much to regret the lack of men filled with the Holy Ghost and with fire.

Men With Apostolic Zeal

In the first place, we have not men with apostolic zeal. Converted in a most singular way, by a direct interposition from heaven, Paul, from that time forward became an earnest man. He had always been earnest, in his sin and in his persecutions; but after he heard that voice from heaven, *"Saul, Saul, why persecutest thou me?"* and had received the mighty office of an apostle, and had been sent forth a chosen vessel to the Gentiles, you can scarce conceive the deep, the awful earnestness which he manifested. Whether he did eat, or drink, or whatsoever he did, he did all for the glory of his God; he never wasted an hour; he was employing his time either in ministering with his own hands unto his necessities, or else lifting those hands in the synagogue, on Mars' Hill, or anywhere where he could command the attention of the multitude. His zeal was so earnest, and so burning, that he could not (as we unfortunately do) restrain himself within a little sphere; but he preached the Word everywhere. It was not enough for him to have it handed down that he was the Apostle of Pisidia, but he must go also to Pamphylia; it was not enough that he should be the great preacher of Pamphylia and Pisidia, but he must go also to Attalia; and when he had preached throughout all Asia, he must needs take ship to Greece, and preach there also.

I believe not once only did Paul hear in his dream the men of Macedonia saying, *"Come over and help us,"* but every day and hour he heard the cry in his ears from multitudes of souls, "Paul, Paul, come over and help us." He could not restrain himself from preaching. *"Woe is unto me,"* he said, *"if I preach not the gospel. God forbid that I should glory save in the cross of Christ."*

Oh! If you could have seen Paul preach, you would not have gone away as you do from some of us, with half a conviction, that we do not mean what we say. His eyes preached a sermon without his lips, and his lips preached it, not in a cold and frigid manner, but every word fell with an overwhelming power upon the hearts of his hearers. He preached with power, because he was in downright earnest. You had a conviction, when you saw him, that he was a man who felt he had a work to do and must do it, and could not contain himself unless he did do it. He was the kind of preacher whom you would expect to see walk down the pulpit stairs straight into his coffin, and then stand before his God, ready for his last account. Where are the men like that man? I confess I cannot claim that privilege, and I seldom hear a solitary sermon which comes up to the mark in earnest, deep, passionate longing for the souls of men.

We have no eyes now like the eyes of the Saviour, which could weep over Jerusalem; we have few voices like that earnest impassioned voice which seemed perpetually to cry, *"Come unto me, and I will give you rest. O Jerusalem, Jerusalem, how often would I have gathered thee as a hen gathereth her chickens under her wings, but ye would not."* If ministers of the gospel were more hearty in their work of preaching; if, instead of giving lectures and devoting a large part of their time to literary and political pursuits, they would preach the Word of God, and preach it as if they were pleading for their own lives, ah! then, my brethren, we might expect great success; but we cannot expect it while we go about our work in a half-hearted way, and have not that zeal, that earnestness, that deep purpose which characterized those men of old.

Men With Apostolic Faith in the Word of God

Then, again, I take it we have not men in our days who can preach like Paul—as to their faith. What did Paul do? He went to Philippi; did he know a soul there? Not one. He had his Master's truth, and he believed in the power of it. He was unattended and devoid of pomp, or show, or parade; he did not go to a pulpit with a soft cushion in it to address a respectable congregation, but he walked through the streets and began to preach to the people. He went to Corinth, to Athens, alone, single-handed, to tell the people the gospel of the blessed God. Why? Because he had faith in the gospel and believed it would save souls and hurl down idols from their thrones.

He had no doubt about the power of the gospel; but now-a-days, my brethren, we have not faith in the gospel we preach. How many there are who preach the gospel, which they are afraid will not save souls; and, therefore, they add little bits of their own to it in order, as they think, to win men to Christ! I hold that a man who does not believe his gospel to be able to save men's souls does not believe it all. If God's truth will not save men's souls, man's lies cannot; if God's truth will not turn men to repentance, I am sure there is nothing in this world that can. When we believe the gospel to be powerful, then we shall see it is powerful. If I walk into this pulpit and say, "I know what I preach is true," the world says I am an egotist. "The young man is dogmatical." Ay, and the young man means to be; he glories in it, he keeps it to himself as one of his peculiar titles, for he does most firmly believe what he preaches.

God forbid that I should ever come tottering up the pulpit stairs to teach anything I was not quite sure of, something which I hoped might save sinners, but of which I was not exactly certain. When I have faith in my doctrines, those doctrines will prevail, for confidence is the winner of the palm. He who hath courage enough to grasp the standard and hold it up, will be sure enough to find followers.

He who says, "I know," and asserts it boldly in his Master's name, without disputing, will not be long before he will find men who will listen to what he says, and who will say, "This man speaks with authority, and not as the Scribes and Pharisees." That is one reason why we do not succeed: we have not faith in the gospel. We send educated men to India in order to confound the learned Brahmins. Nonsense! Let the Brahmins say what they like, have we any business to dispute with them? "Oh, but they are so intellectual and so clever." What have we to do with that?

We are not to seek to be clever in order to meet them. Leave the men of the world to combat their metaphysical errors; we have merely to say, *"This is truth: he that believeth it shall be saved, and he that denieth it shall be damned."* We have no right to come down from the high ground of divine authoritative testimony; and until we maintain that ground, and come out as we ought to do, girded with the belt of divinity—preaching not what may be true, but asserting that which God has most certainly revealed—we shall not see success.

Brethren, I take it we have not the faith of our fathers. I feel myself a poor driveling thing in point of faith. Why, methought sometimes I could believe anything; but now a little difficulty comes before me, I am timid, and I fear. It is when I preach with unbelief in my heart that I preach unsuccessfully; but when I preach with faith and can say, "I know my God has said, that in the self-same hour He will give me what I shall preach, and careless of man's esteem, I preach what I believe to be true," then it is that God owns faith and crowns it with His own crown.

Men With Apostolic Self-Denial

Again: we have not enough self-denial, and that is one reason why we do not prosper. Far be it from me to say aught against the self-denial of those worthy brethren who have left their country to cross the stormy deep and preach the Word.

We hold them to be men who are to be had in honour; but still I ask, where is the self-denial of the apostles now-a-days? I think one of the greatest disgraces that ever was cast upon the church in these days was that last mission to Ireland. Men went over to Ireland, but like men who have valour's better part, brave bold men, they came back again, which is about all we can say of the matter. Why do they not go there again? Why, they say the Irish "hooted" at them. Now, don't you think you see Paul taking a microscope out of his pocket, and looking at the little man who should say to him, "I shall not go there to preach because the Irish hooted me?" "What!" he says, "is this a preacher?—what a small edition of a minister he must be, to be sure!"

"Oh! But they threw stones at us; you have no idea how badly they treated us!" Just tell that to the apostle Paul. I am sure you would be ashamed to do so. "Oh! but in some places the police interfered and said that we should only create a riot." What would Paul have said to that? The police interfering! I did not know that we had any right to care about governments.

Our business is to preach the Word, and if we must be put in the stocks there let us lie; there would come no hurt of it at last. "Oh! But they might have killed some of us." That is just it. Where is that zeal which counted not its life dear so that it might win Christ? I believe that the killing of a few of our ministers would have prospered Christianity. However we might mourn over it, and none more than myself, I say the murder of a dozen of them would have been no greater ground for grief than the slaughter of our men by hundreds in a successful fight for hearths and homes. I would count my own blood most profitably shed in so holy a struggle.

How did the gospel prosper aforetime? Were there not some who laid down their lives for it; and did not others walk to victory over their slain bodies; and must it not be so now? If we are to start back because we are afraid of being killed, heaven knows when the gospel is to spread over the world—we do not. What have other missionaries done? Have they not braved death in its direst forms and preached the Word amid countless dangers?

My brethren, we say again, we find no fault, for we, ourselves, might err in the same manner; but we are sure we are therein not like Paul. He went to a place where they stoned him with stones and dragged him out as dead. Did he say, "Now for the future I will not go where they will ill-treat me"? No, for he says, *"Of the Jews five times received I forty stripes save one. Thrice was I beaten with rods, thrice I suffered shipwreck."*

I am sure we have not the self-denial of the apostles. We are mere carpet-knights and Hyde-park-warriors. When I go to my own house and think how comfortable and happy I am, I say to myself, "How little I do for my Master! I am ashamed that I cannot deny myself for His truth, and go everywhere preaching His Word." I look with pity upon people who say "Do not preach so often; you will kill yourself." O my God! What would Paul have said to such a thing as that? "Take care of your constitution; you are rash; you are enthusiastic." When I compare myself with one of those men of old, I say, "Oh that men should be found calling themselves Christians, who seek to stop our work of faith and labour of love, for the sake of a little consideration about the 'constitution,' which gets all the stronger for the preaching of God's Word."

But I hear some one whispering, "You ought to make a little allowance." My dear friend, I make all allowance. I am not finding fault with those brethren; they are a good sort of people; we are "all honorable men;" but I will only say, that in comparison with Paul, we are less than nothing, and vanity; little insignificant Lilliputian creatures, who can hardly be seen in comparison with those gigantic men of old.

One of my hearers may perhaps hint that this is not the sole cause, and he observes, "I think you ought to make excuse, for ministers now cannot work miracles." Well, I have considered that too, and certainly it is a drawback, but, I take it, not a very great one; for if it had been, God would not have allowed it to exist. He gave that gift to the Church in its infancy, but now it needs it no longer. We mistake in attributing too much to miracles. What was one of them? Wherever the apostles went they could speak the language of the people. Well, in the time it would have taken Paul to walk from here to Hindostan, we could learn Hindustani, and we can go over in a very little time by the means of traveling that are now provided: so that is no great gain there.

Then, again, in order to make the gospel known amongst the people, it was necessary that miracles should be worked, so that every one might talk about it; but now there is a printing press to aid us. What I say today, within six months will be read across the Alleghenies; and so with other ministers, what they say and what they do can soon be printed off and distributed everywhere; so they have facilities for making themselves known which are not much behind the power of miracles. Again, we have a great advantage over the apostles. Wherever they went they were persecuted and sometimes put to death; but now, although occasionally we hear of the massacre of a missionary, the occurrence is rare enough.

The slaughter of an Englishman anywhere would provoke a fleet of men-of-war to visit the offence with chastisement. The world respects an Englishman wherever he goes; he has the stamp of the great Caesar upon him; he is the true cosmopolite—the citizen of the world. That could not be said of the poor despised Jews. There might be some respect paid to Paul, for he was a Roman citizen, but there would be none paid to the rest. We cannot be put to death now without a noise being made. The murder of two or three ministers in Ireland would provoke a tumult through the country; the government would have to interpose, the orderly of the land would be up in arms, and then we might preach with an armed constabulary around us, and so go through the land, provoking the priests, startling antichrist, and driving superstition to its dens for ever.

Second, We Do Not Go About Our Work in an Apostolic Style

There is a general complaint that there is not enough preaching by ministers and missionaries. They sit down interpreting, establishing schools, and doing this, that, and the other. We have nothing to find fault with in this; but that is not the labour to which they should devote themselves; their office is preaching, and if they preached more, they might hope for more success. The missionary Chamberlain preached once at a certain place, and years afterwards disciples were found there from that one sermon. Williams preached wherever he went, and God blessed him; Moffat preached wherever he went, and his labours were owned.

Proclaiming the Priority of Preaching

Now we have our churches, our printing presses, about which a great deal of money is spent. This is doing good, but it is not doing the good. We are not using the means which God has ordained, and we cannot therefore expect to prosper. Some say there is too much preaching now a days, in England. Well, it is the tendency of the times to decry preaching, but it is *"the foolishness of preaching"* which is to change the world. It is not for men to say, "If you preached less, you might study more." Study is required well enough if you have a settled church; but the apostles needed no study, I apprehend, but they stood up and delivered out the simple cardinal truths of religion, not taking one text, but going through the whole catalogue of truth.

So I think, in itinerant evangelical labours, we are not bound to dwell on one subject, for then we need to study, but we shall find it profitable to deal out the whole truth wherever we go. Thus we should always find words to hand, and truths ever ready to teach the people.

Affirming the Divinity of the Gospel

In the next place I conceive that a great mistake has been made in not affirming the divinity of our mission and standing fast by the truth, as being a revelation not to be proved by men, but to be believed; always holding out this, *"He that believeth and is baptized shall be saved; he that believeth not shall be damned."*

I am often grieved when I read of our missionaries holding disputes with the Brahmins, and it is sometimes said that the missionary has beaten the Brahmin because he kept his temper, and so the gospel had gained great honour by the dispute. I take it that the gospel was lowered by the controversy. I think the missionary should say, "I am come to tell you something which the one God of heaven and earth hath said, and I tell you before I announce it, that if you believe it you shall be saved, and if not, you shall be damned. I am come to tell you that Jesus Christ, the Son of God, became flesh, to die for poor unworthy man, that through His mediation, and death, and suffering, the people of God might be delivered. Now, if you will listen to me you shall hear the Word of God: if you do not, I shake the dust of my feet against you, and go somewhere else." Look at the history of every imposture; it shows us that the claim of authority insures a degree of progress. How did Mohammed come to have so strong a religion in his time? He was all alone, and he went into the market-place and said, "I have received a revelation from heaven." It was a lie, but he persuaded men to believe it. People looked at his face; they saw that he looked upon them earnestly as believing what he said, and some five or six of them joined him. Did he prove what he said? Not he. "You must," he said, "believe what I say, or there is no Paradise for you." There is power in that kind of thing, and wherever he went his statement was believed, not on the ground of reasoning, but on his authority, which he declared to be from Allah; and in a century after he first proclaimed his imposture, a thousand sabers had flashed from a thousand sheaths, and his word had been proclaimed through Africa, Turkey, Asia, and even in Spain. The man claimed authority—he claimed divinity; therefore he had power.

Take again the increase of Mormonism. What has been its strength? Simply this—the assertion of power from heaven. That claim is made, and the people believe it, and now they have missionaries in almost every country of the habitable globe, and the book of Mormon is translated into many languages. Though there never could be a delusion more transparent, or a counterfeit less skillful, and more lying upon the very surface, yet this simple pretension to power has been the means of carrying power with it.

Now, my brethren, we have power; we are God's ministers; we preach God's truth; the great Judge of heaven and earth has told us the truth, and what have we to do to dispute with worms of the dust? Why should we tremble and fear them? Let us stand out and say, "We are the servants of the living God; we tell unto you what God has told us, and we warn you, if you reject our testimony, it shall be better for Tyre and Sidon in the day of judgment than for you." If the people cast that away, we have done our work. We have nothing to do with making men believe; ours is to testify of Christ everywhere, to preach and to proclaim the gospel to all men.

We might give up all the books that have been written in defense of Christianity if we would but preach Christ, if, instead of defending the outposts, we were to say, "God will take care of them," and were at once to make a sortie on the enemy; then by God's Holy Spirit we should carry everything before us. O, Church of God! Believe thyself invincible, and thou art invincible; but stay to tremble, and fear, and thou art undone. Lift up thy head and say, "I am God's daughter; I am Christ's bride." Do not stop to prove it, but affirm it; march through the land, and kings and princes shall bow down before thee, because, thou hast taken thine ancient prowess and assumed thine ancient glory.

Employing the Method of Itinerancy

I have one more remark to make here with regard to the style in which we go to work. I fear that we have not enough of the divine method of itinerancy. Paul was a great itinerant: he preached in one place, and there were twelve converted there; he made a church at once; he did not stop till he had five hundred; but when he had twelve, he went off to another place. A holy woman takes him in; she has a son and daughter; they are saved and baptized—there is another church. Then he goes on; wherever he goes the people believe and are baptized, wherever he meets a family who believes, he or his companion baptizes all the house, and goes about his way still forming churches and appointing elders over them.

We, now-a-days, go and settle in a place, make a station of it, and work around it by little and little, and think that is the way to succeed. No, no! Ravage a continent; attempt great things and great things shall be done. But they say if you just pass over a place it will be forgotten like the summer shower, which moistens all, but satisfies none. Yes, but you do not know how many of God's elect may be there; you have no business to stop in one place; go straight on; God's elect are everywhere.

If I could not itinerate this country of England, I could not bear to preach. If I preached here always, many of you would become gospel hardened. I love to go ranging here, there, and everywhere. My highest ambition is this, that I may be found going through the entire land, as well as holding my headquarters in one position. I do hold that itinerancy is God's great plan. There should be fixed ministers and pastors, but those who are like apostles should itinerate far more than they do.

Third, We Have Not Apostolic Churches

This will strike home to some of us. Oh! Had you seen an apostolic church, what a different thing it would appear to one of our churches! as different, I had almost said, as light from darkness, as different as the shallow bed of the brook that is dried by summer is from the mighty rolling river, ever full, ever deep and clear, and ever rushing into the sea.

Now, where is our prayerfulness compared with theirs? I trust that we know something of the power of prayer here, but I do not think we pray like they did. *"They broke bread from house to house, and did eat their meat with singleness of heart, giving glory to God."* There was not a member of the Church, as a rule, who was half-hearted; they gave their souls wholly to God; and when Ananias and Sapphira divided the price, they were smitten with death for their sin. Oh! If we prayed as deeply and as earnestly as they did, we should have as much success. Any measure of success we may have had here has been entirely owing under God to your prayers; and wherever I have gone, I have boasted that I have a praying people. Let other ministers have as prayerful a people; let missionaries have as many prayers from the Church, and, all things being equal, God will bless them, and there will be greater prosperity than ever.

In Liberality

We have not the apostolic mode of liberality. In the apostles' days they gave all their substance. It was not demanded of them then, and it is not now, no one thinks of asking such a thing; still we have run to the other extreme, and many give nothing at all. Men who have thousands and tens of thousands are so eternally considerate for their families, albeit they are provided for, that they give nothing more than the servant girl who sits next to them. It is a common saying, that members of Christian churches do not give in proportion to their wealth.

We give because it is genteel and respectable. A great many of us give I hope, because we love the cause of God; but many of us say, "There is a poor bricklayer, working hard all the week and only earning just enough to keep his wife and family: he will give a shilling; now, I have so many pounds a week—I am a rich man—what shall I give? Why, I will give half-a-crown." Another says, "I will give ten shillings this morning." Now, if they measured their wealth in comparison with his, they would see that he gives all he has left above his maintenance, while they give comparatively nothing.

My brethren, we are not half Christians; that is the reason why we have not half success. We are Christianized, but I question whether we are thoroughly so. The Spirit of God hath not entered into us to give us that life, and fire, and soul, which they had in these ancient times.

Fourth, We Have Not the Holy Spirit in That Measure Which Attended the Apostles

I see no reason whatever, why, this morning, if God willed it, I should not stand up and preach a sermon which should be the means of converting every soul in the place. I see no reason why I should not, tomorrow, preach a sermon which should be the means of the salvation of all who heard it, if God the Spirit were poured out. The Word is able to convert, just as extensively as God the Spirit pleases to apply it; and I can see no reason why, if converts come in by ones and twos now, there should not be a time when hundreds and thousands shall come to God. The same sermon which God blesses to ten if He pleased He could bless to a hundred.

I am sure the Holy Spirit is able to make the Word successful, and the reason why we do not prosper is that we have not the Holy Spirit attending us with might and energy as they had then. My brethren, if we had the Holy Spirit upon our ministry, it would signify very little about our talent. Men might be poor and uneducated; their words might be broken and ungrammatical; there might be no polished periods of Hall, or glorious thunders of Chalmers; but if there were the might of the Spirit attending them, the humblest evangelists would be more successful than the most pompous of divines, or the most eloquent of preachers. It is extraordinary grace, not talent, that wins the day; extraordinary spiritual power, not extraordinary mental power. Mental power may fill a chapel; but spiritual power fills the Church. Mental power may gather a congregation; spiritual power will save souls. We want spiritual power.

Oh! We know some before whom we shrink into nothing as to talent, but who have no spiritual power, and when they speak they have not the Holy Spirit with them; but we know others, simple hearted worthy men who speak their country dialect, and who stand up to preach in their country place, and the Spirit of God clothes every word with power; hearts are broken, souls are saved, and sinners are born again. Spirit of the living God, we want thee. Thou art the life, the soul; Thou art the source of Thy people's success; without Thee they can do nothing, with Thee they can do everything.

Thus I have tried to show you what I conceive to be the causes of our partial non-success. And now permit me, with all earnestness, to plead with you on behalf of Christ and Christ's holy gospel, that you would stir yourselves up to renewed efforts for the spread of His truth, and to more earnest prayers, that His kingdom may come, and His will be done on earth even as it is in heaven.

Ah! My friends, could I show you the tens of thousands of spirits who are now walking in outer darkness; could I take you to the gloomy chamber of hell, and show you myriads upon myriads of heathen souls in utterable torture, not having heard the Word, but being justly condemned for their sins; methinks you could ask yourselves, "Did I do anything to save these unhappy myriads? They have been damned, and can I say I am clear of their blood?" Oh! God of mercy, if these skirts be clear of my fellow creatures' blood, I shall have eternal reason to bless Thee in heaven. Oh! Church of Christ, thou hast great reason to ask thyself whether thou art quite clean in this matter. Ye say too often, ye sons of God, *"Am I my brother's keeper?"*

Ye are too much like Cain; ye do not ask yourselves whether God will require your fellow-creatures' blood at your hands.

Oh! There is a truth which says, *"If the watchman warn them not, they shall perish, but their blood will He require at the watchman's hands."* Ah! there ought to be more of us who are preaching to the heathen, and yet, perhaps, we are indolent and doing little or nothing. There are many of you, yea all of you, who ought to be doing far more than you are for evangelical purposes and the spread of Christ's gospel.

Oh! Put this question to your hearts; shall I be able to say to the damned spirit if he meets me in hell, "Sinner, I did all I could for thee"? I am afraid some will have to say, "No, I did not; it is true I might have done more; I might have laboured more, even though I might have been unsuccessful, but I did not do it." Ah, my dear friends, I believe there is a great reason for some of us to suspect whether we believe our religion at all. An infidel once met a Christian. "Because," said the other, "for years you have passed me on my way to my house of business. You believe, do you not, there is a hell, into which men's spirits are cast?" "Yes, I do," said the Christian. "And you believe that unless I believe in Christ I must be sent there?" "Yes." "You do not, I am sure, because if you did you must be a most inhuman wretch to pass me, day by day, and never tell me about it or warn me of it."

I do hold that there are some Christians who are verily guilty in this matter; God will forgive them, the blood of Christ can even wash that out, but they are guilty. Did you ever think of the tremendous value of a single soul? My hearers, if there were but one man in Siberia unsaved, and all the world were saved besides, if God should move our minds, it would be worth while for all the people in England to go after that one soul. Did you ever think of the value of a soul? Ah! ye have not heard the howls and yells of hell; ye have not heard the mighty songs and hosannas of the glorified; ye have no notion of what eternity is, or else ye would know the value of a soul.

Ye who have been broken by conviction, humbled by the Spirit, and led to cry for mercy through the covenant Jesus; ye know something of what a soul's value is, but many of my hearers do not. Could we preach carelessly, could we pray coldly, if we knew what a precious thing it is about which we are concerned? No, surely we should be doubly in earnest that God will please to save sinners.

I am sure the present state of affairs cannot go on long; we are doing next to nothing; Christianity is at a low ebb. People think it will never be much better; that it is clearly impossible to do wonders in these days. Are we in a worse condition than the Roman Catholic nations were when one man, Luther, preached? Then God can find a Luther now. We are not in a much worse state than when Whitfield began to preach, and yet God can find His Whitfields now.

It is a delusion to suppose that we cannot succeed as they did. God helping us we will; God helping us by His Spirit we will see greater things than this, at any rate, we will never let God's Church rest if we do not see it prosper, but we will enter our earnest hearty protest against the coldness and lethargy of the times, and as long as this our tongue shall move in our mouth, we will protest against the laxity and false doctrine so rampant throughout the Churches, and then that happy double reformation—a reformation in doctrine and Spirit, will be brought about together. Then God knoweth but what we shall say, "Who are these that fly as a cloud, and as the doves to their windows," and ere long the shout of Christ shall be heard. He, Himself, shall descend from heaven; and we shall hear it said and sung, "Alleluia! Alleluia! Alleluia! The Lord God Omnipotent reigneth."

I

The First Century Church

ou did not say, "May I?" When I was just a boy, we often played a game where someone gave instructions to us in an authoritative voice and we obeyed the instructions. For example, we were told to take one giant step. But always before moving forward, we had to ask, "May I?"

If you have started to read this chapter and have taken a giant step over the introduction, you have not asked, "May I?" In the childhood game, we would have been asked to go back to the beginning. I want you to go back to the introduction. You will understand the intent of this book so much more clearly if you take time to read what I have included in the introduction. You will find a message by Charles Spurgeon. As you read it, I trust you will hunger and thirst for first century Christianity. What you find in the next paragraph will be waiting for you just as soon as you return from reading Mr. Spurgeon's message.

Chapter One

Now that you have finished the introduction, you are ready to begin with chapter one.

It is our responsibility to rightly divide God's Word as we deal with what the Bible says about the Jew, the Gentile, and the church. What we believe about the church must come from the Bible. The Bible is our sole authority for faith and practice in the New Testament church.

Our philosophy must come out of our theology. What we believe as Christians must come from what we know to be true about God.

Our philosophy must come out of our theology. What we believe as Christians must come from what we know to be true about God. In other words, it is disastrous to develop a philosophy for life without building that philosophy on the right theological foundation.

The Lord Jesus said, *"I will build my church."* The word translated *"church"* is very significant because it is never used in the Bible to describe a denomination or to describe a national church. The Bible teaches that every church is to be directly accountable to God.

A very simple definition of a local church is a group of baptized believers who have voluntarily joined themselves together to carry out the Great Commission. This is about as simply as one can state it.

In Matthew 16:13, the Lord Jesus asked His disciples when He came to the coast of Caesarea Philippi, *"Whom do men say that I the Son of man am?"*

Someone answered, *"Some say that thou art John the Baptist."*

No doubt when the people heard Him thundering forth the Word of God with such mighty authority they said, "This has to be none other than John the Baptist."

They said, "Some say Elijah." When they saw the miracles of the Lord Jesus, they thought, "This is a prophet of miracles. This must be Elijah." But He was not Elijah.

They said, "Some say Jeremiah." No doubt when the people saw the tears of Jesus Christ, our weeping Savior, they thought of the tender compassion and tears of the prophet Jeremiah.

Then the Lord Jesus asked His disciples in verse fifteen, *"But whom say ye that I am?"*

Simon Peter stepped forward and said, *"Thou art the Christ, the Son of the living God."*

The Lord Jesus took that statement and said in verse eighteen, *"Upon this rock I will build my church; and the gates of hell shall not prevail against it."* His church is His called-out assembly. As we read this statement, we can place the emphasis in any number of places. Let us emphasize *"I will."* The Lord will get it done. The church has many enemies and critics, but Jesus Christ is everlastingly at it. He is building His church.

It is important for us to note that the Lord Jesus said, *"I will build my church."*

He did not say, "I will build *your* church." He did not say, "You will build *my* church." He said, *"I will build my church."* Those who seek to market the church and practice "anything to get people to come" want to tell us that it is our business to be church builders. No, God gives the increase. He builds the church. We have one responsibility, and that is to be obedient to the Lord. As we obey the Lord, the Lord will build His church.

We have one responsibility, and that is to be obedient to the Lord. As we obey the Lord, the Lord will build His church.

The following is from one of Charles Haddon Spurgeon's warnings against "the Downgrade" in doctrine and the deep evangelical disobedience of his day, especially in the Baptist Union.

The article was entitled "Progressive Theology" and was published in *The Sword and the Trowel*, April, 1888:

> But what if earnest protests accomplish nothing, because of the invincible resolve of the infatuated to abide in fellowship with the inventors of false doctrine? Well, we shall at least have done our duty. We are not responsible for success. If the plague cannot be stayed, we can at least die in the attempt to remove it.

We are not responsible for success.
–Charles Spurgeon

> Every voice that is lifted up against Anythingarianism is at least a little hinderance to its universal prevalence. It may be that in some one instance a true witness is strengthened by our word, or a waverer is kept from falling; and this is no mean reward. It is true that our testimony may be held up to contempt; and may, indeed, in itself be feeble enough to be open to ridicule; but yet the Lord, by the weak things of the world, has overcome the mighty in former times, and he will do so again.... Assuredly, the conflict to which the faithful are now summoned is not less arduous than that in which the Reformers were engaged. So much of subtilty is mixed up with the whole business, that the sword seems to fall upon a sack of wool, or to miss its mark. However, plain truth will cut its way in the end, and policy will ring its own death-knell."

The Lord is doing His work in this world through local churches. The pastor of a New Testament church needs to help people understand how they can serve the Lord by finding their place of service in the local church.

The Lord Jesus said, *"I will build my church."*

The First Century Church Started With Christ and His Disciples and Was Empowered at Pentecost

We need to know some basic things concerning the local church. The church started with Christ and His disciples and was empowered at Pentecost.

When I was a seminary student, I was given the assignment of writing a rather long paper concerning when the church started. In my research, I discovered more than a dozen different ideas concerning when the church began.

From my own study of God's Word, I have come to the conviction that the church started with Christ and His disciples and was empowered at Pentecost. Through the centuries, a great host has taken this same position. When we come to this conclusion, we realize what the Lord assigned to the church, not simply to a group of believers. The ordinances of the church, baptism and the Lord's Supper, are not ministerial ordinances; they are local church ordinances.

Consider what we find in Matthew chapter eighteen. When the Lord Jesus speaks again of the church in verses fifteen through seventeen, He says,

> *Moreover if thy brother shall trespass against thee, go and tell him his fault between thee and him alone: if he shall hear thee, thou hast gained thy brother.*

> *But if he will not hear thee, then take with thee one or two more, that in the mouth of two or three witnesses every word may be established. And if he shall neglect to hear them, tell it unto the church: but if he neglect to hear the church, let him be unto thee as a heathen man and a publican.*

The so-called "invisible church" would have a hard time hearing this matter. The Lord said, *"my church."* This is an organized group that the Lord said one could speak to, and when necessary, exercise church discipline within.

The First Century Church Had a Saved Membership

Another thing that Christians should know about the New Testament church is that the church had a saved membership. In Acts 2:41-42 the Bible says,

> *Then they that gladly received his word were baptized: and the same day there were added unto them about three thousand souls. And they continued stedfastly in the apostles' doctrine and fellowship, and in breaking of bread, and in prayers.*

Here we read of those who *"gladly received his word"* and obeyed the Lord in baptism. When you ask a man if he is saved, he may tell you that he truly knows Christ as his Savior but does not belong to a local church. From the record we find in Scripture, those who came to know Christ as Savior obeyed Him in baptism and identified themselves with a local assembly of believers.

From the example we find in the Bible, we learn that people "joined" the local body of believers. Acts 9:26 speaks of Paul joining himself to the church. Not only should we be Christians, we should be obedient to Christ in believer's baptism and belong to a local, Bible-believing, Bible-preaching church. Each one of us should place his life and influence with other believers who have voluntarily joined themselves together to carry out the Great Commission. As God gives us health and strength, we should faithfully attend the services of the church and support the work of the Lord through that local church with our prayers, finances, and labors of love.

From this passage, we learn that those who were added to the church were saved and followed the Lord in baptism. Also, there was a body of doctrine connected with this church. They continued steadfastly in the apostles' doctrine. Each member was committed to this body of doctrine.

In order for baptism to be biblically correct, there must first be the right authority, which is the local church. The Lord gave this authority to the local church.

The Lord Jesus said in Matthew 28:19-20, *"Go ye therefore, and teach all nations, baptizing them in the name of the Father, and of the Son, and of the Holy Ghost: teaching them to observe all things whatsoever I have commanded you."*

When Christ gave the command for believers to be baptized, He spoke to the local church.

Second, there must be the right mode of baptism, which is immersion. Immersion is going into the water, under the water, and up out of the water. Immersion is the only mode of baptism that pictures our death with the Lord Jesus Christ, our burial with the Lord Jesus Christ, and the new life we have in Christ. According to Romans chapter six, not only did our Lord die *for* us, He died *as* us. He took our place.

Third, there must be the right candidate for baptism. This is a person who truly knows the Lord Jesus Christ as Savior. People must be saved before they follow the Lord in baptism. This is why we use the term "believer's baptism."

The First Century Church Had Christ as the Only Head

Another thing we need to know about the local church is that Christ is the only head of the church.

The Bible says in Colossians 1:18, *"And he is the head of the body, the church: who is the beginning, the firstborn from the dead; that in all things he might have the preeminence."*

A New Testament church recognizes that it only has one headquarters, and that is heaven. The church has only one head, and that is the Lord Jesus.

The body of doctrine that the Lord Jesus gave to His disciples when He established the church is the same body of doctrine that we earnestly contend for today. We trace our roots to the Lord Jesus and His disciples knowing that, throughout the centuries, God has always had a people who believed the same body of doctrine that Christ gave to His disciples.

We have a Book, the completed revelation of God, the Bible, and winding through the centuries, people have had the same body of doctrine to hand to the next generation.

Our faith was once delivered, but it must be contended for in every generation. The Bible says in Jude 3,

> *Beloved, when I gave all diligence to write unto you of the common salvation, it was needful for me to write unto you, and exhort you that ye should earnestly contend for the faith which was once delivered unto the saints.*

Some think Jude took pen in hand and had a desire to write about the common salvation, but God directed him differently. This is exactly opposite of what this passage teaches.

The writer, the human penman God used, explained in dealing with the common salvation, *"It was needful for me to write unto you to earnestly contend for the faith."* We lose the message unless we *"contend for the faith."* We are going to answer to the Lord Jesus for this matter of contending for the faith. If we do not *"earnestly contend for the faith,"* we will not be giving the same message to the next generation.

No one and no thing is to take the place of Jesus Christ as head of the church. This will take care of the idea of denominationalism. I gladly identify myself as a member of a Baptist church, but we must never allow denominationalism to take the place of Jesus Christ as head of the church. The Lord Jesus is the only head of the New Testament church.

The First Century Church Was Declared to Be the Pillar and Ground of the Truth

The Bible teaches that the church is *"the pillar and ground of the truth."* The Bible says in I Timothy 3:15-16,

> *But if I tarry long, that thou mayest know how thou oughtest to behave thyself in the house of God, which is the church of the living God, the pillar and ground of the truth. And without controversy great is the mystery of godliness: God was manifest in the flesh, justified in the Spirit, seen of angels, preached unto the Gentiles, believed on in the world, received up into glory.*

Chapter One

Often people assign some responsibility to the church that is not a biblical assignment. Using the very words of Scripture, the church is *"the pillar and ground of the truth."*

I like the imagery God uses when He says, *"The pillar and ground of the truth."* We are taking the truth to people in every generation. Think what a staggering responsibility we have in our churches to be *"the pillar and ground of the truth."*

In our world, we have traded truth for tolerance. Millions refuse to have any fixed point of reference. The local church is to be *"the pillar and ground of the truth."* The fixed point of reference is the Word of God, which is the sole authority for our faith and practice.

In our world, there is no lack of knowledge, but there is a great lack of truth. We live in an information age, and we are bombarded, overloaded, and absolutely overwhelmed with knowledge; but it is truth we need. We must lift up the truth in love.

THE FIRST CENTURY CHURCH WAS ALWAYS AN INDEPENDENT CONGREGATION

The church we find in the New Testament was an independent congregation. In Acts thirteen, the great church in Antioch was about to send out missionaries. The Bible says in Acts 13:1-4,

> *Now there were in the church that was at Antioch certain prophets and teachers; as Barnabas, and Simeon that was called Niger, and Lucius of Cyrene, and Manaen, which had been brought up with Herod the tetrarch, and Saul. As they ministered to the Lord, and fasted, the Holy Ghost said, Separate me Barnabas and Saul for the work whereunto I have called them. And when they had fasted and prayed, and laid their*

> *hands on them, they sent them away. So they, being sent forth by the Holy Ghost, departed unto Seleucia; and from thence they sailed to Cyprus.*

The people of the church sent them out, but the Word of God also says the Holy Ghost sent them out. Which is it? Were they sent by the Holy Ghost or sent by the church?

They were sent by both. The church recognized the Spirit of God at work. This local congregation acted independently of any other congregation. As we read about the church in the Bible, we are reading about local, independent congregations. Each congregation was autonomous. They were self-governing. Read your Bible and examine your local church by the Word of God. Each church is to be entirely biblical in its distinctives.

The First Century Church Took Responsibility to Evangelize the World

In Acts 1:8 the Bible says, *"But ye shall receive power, after that the Holy Ghost is come upon you: and ye shall be witnesses unto me both in Jerusalem, and in all Judaea, and in Samaria, and unto the uttermost part of the earth."*

What can one church do in a world of more than six billion people? We need to see our place in God's work to evangelize the world. Just imagine if every local, independent congregation felt responsible for the consuming command given by the Lord to go into all the world and preach the gospel to every creature.

Churches have lost their vision. There is a world of difference between ambition and vision. Ambition is something that comes from men. An ambitious man cannot be helped. He is interested only in doing more to magnify the flesh. Vision is something that comes from God. God gives vision. Our vision leads us to do what God has already stated clearly in His Word that needs to be done. The vision God gives us is always a world vision. When you find a New Testament church, you find a local church that has taken seriously God's command for world evangelism.

It is the responsibility of each local church to start other churches. May God grant us a mighty revival of church planting and send New Testament church pioneers into His harvest field. This church planting revival will not come as a result of making church planting the goal; it will come only as obedience to God is the goal.

THE FIRST CENTURY CHURCH WAS PASTOR-LED

Sheep need a shepherd, and our Lord has designed that the local church be led by a shepherd–their pastor.

This man is not a hireling; he is a shepherd. He loves the sheep and gives his life for the sheep. *"The good shepherd giveth his life for the sheep"* (John 10:11).

I Timothy 3:1 says, *"This is a true saying, If a man desire the office of a bishop, he desireth a good work."* The word *"bishop"* is a word God uses synonymously with *elder* and *shepherd*. These are different terms for the same office. *"Bishop"* means "one who can see and oversee." The man of God should be a man who sees farther than others in the church because God gives him discernment. He is a discerning man who recognizes things earlier than perhaps others recognize them. When little devils pop up, he is going to fight the little devils because he discerns that there is going to be a big devil someday if he does not fight the little ones.

There are battles to be fought. These are tests God brings to prove the pastor. The pastor leads the people as he looks to the Lord.

God enables the pastor. Just as God raised up Joshua in the eyes of the people, the Lord will prove Himself through the pastor to the people of the church as the pastor seeks wisdom from God to deal with the problems. They will recognize that they have God's man to lead them.

We find in I Peter 5:2 that God says to the elders, *"Feed the flock of God which is among you, taking the oversight thereof, not by constraint, but willingly; not for filthy lucre, but of a ready mind."* The pastor is to *feed* the flock and to take the *oversight* thereof.

In Colossian 1:28 we find that the work of the pastor is to *"preach, warning every man, and teaching every man in all wisdom; that we may present every man perfect in Christ Jesus."*

Every New Testament church should be a pastor-led church. There are people you are going to meet in your church who cannot lead and will not follow. This is a tough crowd to handle. But if the pastor will get in the saddle and ride, God will ride with him. If he is able to say honestly before God, "The Lord Jesus is leading us forward," the church will follow. The New Testament church is a pastor-led church.

God's Word gives us a clear pattern from the first century church. Jesus Christ said, *"I will build my church."* Our responsibility is to follow Christ and be obedient to Him. May the Lord help each one of us to find our place of service in the local New Testament church.

II

THE MEASURE OF THE FIRST CENTURY CHURCH

The measure of the first century church was in its likeness to Jesus Christ. The most wonderful thing about a church is its likeness to Jesus Christ. Every thing that is not like Him is an ugly blemish on His body.

We learn much about the first century church in the book of Ephesians. This book is one of the apostle Paul's prison epistles. This epistle was the first to come forth from his imprisonment. Many call this the jewel of the Pauline Epistles.

In Ephesians 4:11-16 the Bible says,

> *And he gave some, apostles; and some, prophets; and some, evangelists; and some, pastors and teachers; for the perfecting of the saints, for the work of the ministry, for the edifying of the body of Christ: till we all come in the unity of the faith, and of the knowledge of the Son of God, unto a perfect man, unto the measure of the stature of the fulness of Christ:*

> *that we henceforth be no more children, tossed to and fro, and carried about with every wind of doctrine, by the sleight of men, and cunning craftiness, whereby they lie in wait to deceive; but speaking the truth in love, may grow up into him in all things, which is the head, even Christ: from whom the whole body fitly joined together and compacted by that which every joint supplieth, according to the effectual working in the measure of every part, maketh increase of the body unto the edifying of itself in love.*

This beautiful passage of Scripture has to do with the church. The Bible speaks of the church as being Christ's body. Every part of the body is to function together.

> *The most wonderful thing about a church is its likeness to Jesus Christ. Every thing that is not like Him is an ugly blemish on His body.*

If the Lord Jesus Christ came and walked on this earth as He once did in bodily form, how would He do it? He has left no room for doubt. He does this through every local assembly of baptized believers who have voluntarily joined themselves together to carry out the Great Commission. As a matter of fact, each New Testament church is His body on this earth.

The Bible says here, in the very words of Scripture, *"Till we all come in the unity of the faith, and of the knowledge of the Son of God, unto a perfect man, unto the measure of the stature of the fulness of Christ."* The Bible says in verses fourteen and fifteen,

> *That we henceforth be no more children, tossed to and fro, and carried about with every wind of doctrine, by the sleight of men, and cunning craftiness, whereby they lie in wait to deceive; but speaking the truth in*

love, may grow up into him in all things, which is the head, even Christ.

The Bible says when we come to the place where we have this unity of the faith, to the measure of the staure of the fullness of Christ, we will no longer act childishly. We are to have child-like faith, but we are not to be childish. We are not going to be blown around in the wind; we are going to be steadfast.

In Galatians chapter four, Paul was wrestling and travailing with things concerning the believers in Galatia. He wrote in Galatians 4:19, *"My little children, of whom I travail in birth again until Christ be formed in you."* He said in verses eight and nine, "I travailed first to see you born again, to get the gospel to you." Now he says, "I'm travailing again that you be delivered from this outward religion. I'm travailing *'until Christ be formed in you.'*"

Paul spoke about the same thing in Ephesians chapter four. He said in verse thirteen, *"unto a perfect man, unto the measure of the stature of the fulness of Christ."* We are to be like Jesus Christ. Every part of life is to be yielded to Him, to be like the Lord Jesus, so that His body functions the way it should function. The measure of our ministry is in our likeness to Jesus Christ.

I often hear pastors say when they have taken a new church, "I'm going to preach to the people about being unified in the Lord. I'm going to speak about unity in the church, about everyone getting along."

I know they have good intentions, but we are not going to find the unity we desire simply because someone preaches that we should have it. There must be a meeting place, a common ground. This common ground is the Person of Jesus Christ.

For example, if you love the Lord Jesus and follow Him and I love the Lord Jesus and follow Him, then we are going to get along and be in unity in the faith. But no matter how hard we work at having unity, no matter how much we push and strive and talk about it, if people do not love the Lord and desire to follow the Lord, there can be no *"unity of the faith."* The unity is not the goal; it is a by-product of giving ourselves as completely as possible to the Lord Jesus Christ.

The same thing is true in marriage. Our oneness is in the Lord Jesus Christ. As a believer, the Lord dwells in my heart. As a believer, the Lord dwells in my wife's heart. When God made us, He made us spirit, soul, and body. In her spirit, the Lord Jesus Christ lives and abides. In my spirit, the Lord Jesus Christ lives and abides. As we deal with differences that are quite natural, we find our unity in the Lord Jesus.

> *The measure of our ministry is in our likeness to Jesus Christ.*

This is what Paul was preaching and teaching. We find our unity in the Person of Jesus Christ as we yield to Him. If you have some difference with someone, think first about what you have in common with him in Christ. Is Christ your Savior? Do you truly know Him? Have you been born again of the Spirit of God?

All of us were dead in our trespasses and sins by nature. We were stillborn spiritually. There must be a time in life when we are born again spiritually. Has this happened in your life? The common ground is in the Person of the Lord Jesus Christ. We can be one in Him. We can be in *"the unity of the faith"* through Him. We can believe what we should believe in Him. We can follow Him, love Him, adore Him, serve Him, worship Him, and come together in this unity of the faith in the Person of Jesus Christ.

He Gave Some Apostles

In order to accomplish God's goal in the local assembly, the Bible says in Ephesians 4:11 that *"he gave some, apostles; and some, prophets; and some, evangelists; and some, pastors and teachers."* The office of an apostle, one qualification of which was to have been an eyewitness to the resurrected Christ, no longer exists. But, as far as being someone sent to witness, as the word *apostle* implies, that is what all of us should be doing. Our Lord Jesus was sent. We are sent. He gave *apostles*.

He Gave Some Prophets

The Bible says He gave *"some, prophets."* As far as being a prophet in the sense that we can *foretell* things that God reveals to us before they ever happen, this no longer exists, because we have the completed, written revelation of the Word of God. But, as far as *forth telling* the Word of God, preaching and declaring God's message, we certainly should be doing that. God gives *prophets*.

He Gave Some Evangelists

The Lord says He not only gave *apostles* and *prophets*, but He also gave *"some, evangelists."* These are people who go with the gospel message into areas where Christ is not known. The work of an evangelist is winning souls and establishing churches. At the earliest point in every local church, the evangelist did his work and someone came to Christ. The Lord gave *evangelists*.

He Gave Some Pastors

Next we find the pastors mentioned. The pastors, the shepherds, care for the flock, loving and leading the people as a shepherd would his sheep. They feed the flock of God. They willingly take the oversight. They serve under the Lord. They lead the local assembly. He gave *pastors*.

He Gave Some Teachers

There is also the ministry of teaching the Word of God. This means explaining the Scripture, line upon line, precept upon precept, comparing Scripture with Scripture, and declaring the Word of God.

These gifts, when put into practice, exemplify the ministry of the Lord Jesus Christ as an *apostle*, a *prophet*, an *evangelist*, a *pastor* and a *teacher*. He was sent by the Father. He preached God's Word. He went after the lost. He pastored His disciples, teaching them how to love and care for others. He taught the Scriptures to His followers.

The work of the ministry cannot be confined to a local meeting of believers inside a building. The work of the ministry should be done every day we live, where we travel, where we work, with the people with whom we have contact.

Our ministry is to continue His ministry. These gifts to the church enable us to continue the ministry of Jesus Christ. Each local assembly when functioning properly represents well the beautiful ministry of the Lord Jesus Christ. Our measure is in our likeness to Him.

The Lord gave these gifts to the church that by these He might accomplish His purpose. The Bible says in verse twelve, *"For the perfecting of the saints, for the work of the ministry, for the edifying of the body of Christ."* He gave these to the church for the perfecting of the saints, which is maturing in the Lord. Are you growing in the grace and knowledge of Jesus Christ? Are you maturing in the Lord?

For the Perfecting of the Saints

We must yield to Christ every area in our lives that is not what it should be. There may be something outwardly that God uses to point to something inward. You may react wrongly to someone in your family or someone on the job; but that is only an indication that there is an area in your life that has not been yielded to Christ. It is like a mirror God uses to help us see that this area needs to be given to God *"for the perfecting of the saints."* This *"perfecting"* is about becoming complete in Christ.

For the Work of the Ministry

He said also, *"for the work of the ministry."* As the saints are perfected, they do the work of the ministry. The work of the ministry must be done on a daily basis. The work of the ministry grows out of the lives of perfected saints.

The work of the ministry cannot be confined to a local meeting of believers inside a building. The work of the ministry should be done every day we live, where we travel, where we work, with the people with whom we have contact.

> *The work of the ministry grows out of the lives of perfected saints.*

The work of the ministry is done as we live for Christ before those people. We must speak to people the way the Lord Jesus would speak to those people. We are to deal with situations as the Lord Jesus would deal with those situations.

For the Edifying of the Body of Christ

Then the Bible says, *"for the edifying of the body of Christ."* This means "building up." The edifying of the body of Christ naturally follows the work of the ministry. Just as surely as you would place stones one upon another to build a structure, God says there are things that should be placed in your life to be built up, to be strengthened as a Christian.

Why? The answer is in verse thirteen, *"Till we all come in the unity of the faith, and of the knowledge of the Son of God, unto a perfect man, unto the measure of the stature of the fulness of Christ."* Christ is our goal. Our goal is God!

Verse fourteen states, *"That we henceforth be no more children, tossed to and fro, and carried about with every wind of doctrine."* This is what God intends in our lives. We must be strong in the Lord.

Each local assembly when functioning properly represents well the beautiful ministry of the Lord Jesus Christ.

How can we take on huge projects and attempt things for God that require great faith? How do we move in one accord to accomplish such things? It is not because someone has a whip and he is driving us. It is not because we want to achieve greatness in the eyes of men. It is because we must take the time to pray, read God's Word, wait on God, and find out what God wants. All of us move forward as believers, believing that Christ desires this of each of us. This is the unity of the faith.

The goal of the pastor is to work toward this. He leads as he follows Christ. It is his responsibility. As Paul wrote to the church in Colosse, the Bible says in Colossians 1:24-28,

> *Who now rejoice in my sufferings for you, and fill up that which is behind of the afflictions of Christ in my flesh for his body's sake, which is the church: whereof I am made a minister, according to the dispensation of God which is given to me for you, to fulfil the word of God; even the mystery which hath been hid from ages and from generations, but now is made manifest to his saints: to whom God would make known what is the riches of the glory of this mystery among the Gentiles; which is Christ in you, the hope of glory: whom we preach, warning every man, and teaching*

every man in all wisdom; that we may present every man perfect in Christ Jesus.

Paul said, "It is my job to warn every man, to teach every man, that every man may be presented perfect in Christ." This is the pastor's responsibility.

Many people have no idea why they come to a church meeting. Sadly, so many pastors could not explain the biblical reason for the meeting of the church. The worst thing imaginable is for them to get the idea that the meeting is an end in itself. People get the idea that they have earned merit just because they came to church.

Why do we assemble together? We assemble together so that we might be perfected. Weak areas of our lives are brought to realization as the Spirit of God convicts us. The light of God's Word and the light of God's Spirit shine on us and show us, "You are not Christ-like in these areas of your life."

We meet together so that we might hear how to do the work of the ministry. We come so that we might be edified and built up, to be strong in the Lord, to have this unity of the faith to go out and do God's work. Of course, we are to be constantly aware of those who are lost and need to hear clearly the way of salvation in the Lord Jesus Christ.

Christ is our goal. Our goal is God!

Many people show up at church and are always checking their watch, looking at the time. They just cannot wait to get out. Apparently, they have not come for the right reason.

There are others who come to be seen. They do not come for the right reason. Some people come and say, "I'm making someone else happy in doing this." They have not come for the right reason.

Chapter Two

When we are truly following the Lord, we come with Bible in hand, with an open heart to the Lord, saying, "Lord, speak to me. Show me. Help me. Reveal to me areas in my life that need to be yielded to Thee. Enable me to do Your work each day, all during the week. Show me how to do the work of the ministry. Help me, Lord, to be built up and to be strong. I don't want to be like a child, blown away by everything that happens. I don't want Satan to have an advantage over me. I don't want to be a childish person, overreacting to everything all week long. Build me up, Lord. Strengthen me. Help me to know how I can be strong in Thee. Help me to leave this place and go out to live the Christian life in a way that demonstrates that Jesus Christ is real, that He is alive and at work in my heart!" We leave the assembly seeking the lost as Christ seeks them through us.

The man of God went, armed with the Word of God and filled with the Spirit of God, to declare the message of God.

Is this what is happening in your life? Whether the meeting is a gathering of many people or a handful of people, when that local assembly of baptized believers who have voluntarily joined themselves together to carry out the Great Commission comes together, it is for a purpose. As a part of a local assembly, it is your responsibility to make sure you are moving toward *"the measure of the stature of the fulness of Christ."*

In our local church we have been together for many years serving God. Our precious people know that we wait on God, we pray, we seek God's way, we try not to get in a hurry. Some may say, "I don't know about all these things you attempt to do," but we still take the time to pray and wait on God and see if God is in it. We wait for the Lord to show us, to give us His direction, and move forward in the unity of the faith.

As we look back at the beginning of the church in Ephesus, we uncover some amazing secrets to all of this. Make note of these secrets.

Three Months in the Synagogue

The Bible records a part of Paul's ministry when he entered the city of Ephesus and preached. In Acts 19:8 the Bible says, *"And he went into the synagogue, and spake boldly for the space of three months, disputing and persuading the things concerning the kingdom of God."*

There he was in Ephesus for three months in the synagogue. There were Jews in Ephesus. Ephesus was a seacoast city, a great commercial city. It was a city with one of the wonders of the world, the temple to the goddess Diana. That temple took two hundred years to build.

Ephesus was a city filled with people who were superstitious. They were very religious, but false religion and idols prevailed. It was a city filled with sorcery and demonic activity. It was a city that greatly resisted the truth of the gospel.

Ephesus was a vital, important city, a gateway to Asia Minor. The man of God went, armed with the Word of God and filled with the Spirit of God, to declare the message of God. In that awful place with all its commercial activity, Paul planted a local church in the first century. The Bible says he spent three months there in the synagogues disputing and persuading. That was not easy work. There he gathered a core group of people who were earnestly seeking the truth.

Two Years in a Rented Hall

The Bible says in Acts 19:9-10,

> *But when divers were hardened, and believed not, but spake evil of that way before the multitude, he departed from them, and separated the disciples,*

disputing daily in the school of one Tyrannus. And this continued by the space of two years; so that all they which dwelt in Asia heard the word of the Lord Jesus, both Jews and Greeks.

The meeting place became a center for evangelizing other areas and starting churches.

Paul spent three months in the synagogue, and the opposition became so intense there that he took the disciples that had been made during those three months, and he rented a hall, the hall of Tyrannus. He stayed there for two years. But we learn that he was not only meeting in that hall; they were launching out from there, preaching the gospel and seeing souls saved, establishing churches in regions round about. The meeting place became a center for evangelizing other areas and starting churches.

A Great Uproar in the City

Satan always opposes the work and the workers of the Lord. In Acts 19:18-20, we read about such an uproar in the city of Ephesus. The Bible says,

> *And many that believed came, and confessed, and shewed their deeds. Many of them also which used curious arts brought their books together, and burned them before all men: and they counted the price of them, and found it fifty thousand pieces of silver. So mightily grew the word of God and prevailed.*

Such an impact was made that they had a great gathering, and people brought all kinds of things to be burned. The Bible mentions books, but no doubt there were different fetishes and idols that were brought also. They piled all these things together in the city of Ephesus and burned them. So that we might have a record of it, someone made note of the price of it all. It was worth fifty thousand pieces of silver.

There was such an uproar that a silversmith who made little idols of the goddess Diana began to say to other silversmiths, "This man is causing such a disturbance. So many people are coming to Christ that our business is suffering. This is a commercial area and we need this business."

The temple of Diana was not only a place of worship; it was also a place of merchandising and business. It was a marketing center in Ephesus. The silversmith said, "The whole city is being impacted by the preaching of this man. We have to get rid of this crowd!" That was the impact of the gospel. The entire city was set in an uproar, but the Lord miraculously delivered His man.

Paul was delivered from Ephesus to continue the mighty work God gave him to do. On his final visit to the area, he sent for the Ephesian elders to bid them farewell.

On this occasion the Lord records for us many helpful things about how the apostle did his work there. He reminds the elders of his time with them and charges them with their responsibilities. This is a tender scene that reminds us of the great love between people and the leader who told them of Christ.

Satan always opposes the work and the workers of the Lord.

When Paul was giving his farewell to these people, notice what the Bible says in Acts 20:24-32,

> *But none of these things move me, neither count I my life dear unto myself, so that I might finish my course with joy, and the ministry, which I have*

> *received of the Lord Jesus, to testify the gospel of the grace of God. And now, behold, I know that ye all, among whom I have gone preaching the kingdom of God, shall see my face no more. Wherefore I take you to record this day, that I am pure from the blood of all men. For I have not shunned to declare unto you all the counsel of God. Take heed therefore unto yourselves, and to all the flock, over the which the Holy Ghost hath made you overseers, to feed the church of God, which he hath purchased with his own blood. For I know this, that after my departing shall grievous wolves enter in among you, not sparing the flock. Also of your own selves shall men arise, speaking perverse things, to draw away disciples after them. Therefore watch, and remember, that by the space of three years I ceased not to warn every one night and day with tears. And now, brethren, I commend you to God, and to the word of his grace, which is able to build you up, and to give you an inheritance among all them which are sanctified.*

Paul said, "For three months I disputed in the synagogues. For two years I hired a hall. For the space of three years I ceased not to warn everyone night and day with tears." He was summarizing his ministry in the city of Ephesus.

Do Not Shun Any of the Counsel of God

Notice that Paul said in Acts 20:27, *"For I have not shunned to declare unto you all the counsel of God."* Do not shun any of the counsel of God.

There are people who want to pick and choose their faith. They say, "That's for some people, but not for me."

Paul said, *"For I have not shunned to declare unto you all the counsel of God."* He said, "I've declared to you what was in the Bible. It is God's Word. I didn't pick and choose. I gave you all of what the Bible says."

We need to be people who do not shun any of the counsel of God. When God deals with us through His Word and by His Spirit about a matter in our lives, then we should say, "This is for me. I am going to heed this. I am going to be obedient to this. This is for my life." We must learn to say yes to Jesus Christ when God speaks to us. We grow in the Lord Jesus as we are obedient to His Word. Strong churches are made of Christians who are strong in the Lord because of their obedience to Him.

Take Heed to Yourself

In verse twenty-eight, Paul gave the admonition, *"Take heed therefore unto yourselves."* We must take heed to ourselves. We must keep ourselves right.

If you will listen carefully to your own words, you will discover something. You will discover that you complain often about what other people are doing. You give more heed to them than you do your own life. God says, "Take heed to yourself. Keep yourself right with God."

In I Timothy 4:16, we read Paul's counsel to Timothy. The Bible says, *"Take heed unto thyself, and unto the doctrine; continue in them: for in doing this thou shalt both save thyself, and them that hear thee."* He said, "Timothy, take heed to thyself. Keep yourself right with God."

There is a limit to what someone else can do for you. You alone are in control of your attitude. Keep yourself right. You are personally accountable to God.

I am willing to try to help people, but it is wonderful when people learn to encourage themselves in the Lord and keep themselves right with God. It is wonderful when people grow up and are no longer so childish that you have to keep them pumped up all the time.

Feed on God's Word Daily

Something else we note that Paul said is also found in verse twenty-eight, *"Take heed therefore unto yourselves, and to all the flock, over the which the Holy Ghost hath made you overseers, to feed the church of God, which he hath purchased with his own blood."* We must feed on God's Word daily.

Strong churches are made of Christians who are strong in the Lord because of their obedience to Him.

We know very little about hunger. Somewhere in this world, twelve thousand people die of hunger every day. One third of the world's population–over two billion people–go to bed hungry every night. The issue is not with the supply of food, but with the distribution of it. The same is true of God's Word.

This Bible is our food, but many of God's children go days without feeding on it. How do you eat it? You do not eat it all at one time. How do you feed on the Word of God?

The Bible says in Isaiah 28:10, *"For precept must be upon precept, precept upon precept; line upon line, line upon line; here a little, and there a little."* We just take one bite at a time. We take a little here, a little there. If we are going to be Christ-like, we must feed on the Word of God.

Read your Bible. Memorize Scripture. Search the Scriptures. Compare Scripture with Scripture. God's Word is our daily food.

Commend All to God

The Bible says in Acts 20:29-32,

> *For I know this, that after my departing shall grievous wolves enter in among you, not sparing the flock. Also of your own selves shall men arise, speaking perverse things, to draw away disciples after them. Therefore watch, and remember, that by the space of three years I ceased not to warn every one night and day with tears. And now, brethren, I commend you to God.*

This matter of "commending to God" involves releasing by faith. Turn loose. Cast your cares on Him; He cares for you. Give your loved ones to God. Help others to recognize their own accountability to God.

We must learn to commend all to God. This means all things and all people. People who are growing in the Lord, who are having Christ formed in them, are people who are commending all to God. They are trusting God with all.

Think how different our lives would be if we would commend all things to God. Paul said, "I'm leaving Ephesus. You will see my face no more. Three years I was there. Two of those years I hired a hall and preached to you. For the first three months I reasoned and persuaded and preached and declared in the synagogues. I love you so, but I'm going now and you will not see me on this earth again."

The Bible describes the scene as one where they wept and cried and embraced. It was an extremely emotional time. How could a man turn loose of those people? Because he said, "I am giving you to One greater than I. I'm commending you to God."

There may be many people or many things in all of our lives that continually disrupt what we are trying to do for the Lord because we simply will not commend them to God. We must give all to God.

We are not to shun any of the counsel of God. We are to take heed to ourselves. We are to feed on God's Word daily. We are taught to commend all to the Lord, to trust God with all things.

These things that Paul recapped in his parting words to the Ephesian elders are the things that help us to become Christians who are growing in Christ-likeness. Do you want this for your life? God has it available for us if we will trust Him. The measure of the first century church was in its likeness to Jesus Christ. How do we measure up to Him?

III

The Power of the First Century Church

In one verse of the New Testament we find the key to unlock the secret of the first century church. It is a matter of God's power.

The Bible says in Acts 1:8, *"But ye shall receive power, after that the Holy Ghost is come upon you: and ye shall be witnesses unto me both in Jerusalem, and in all Judaea, and in Samaria, and unto the uttermost part of the earth."*

This is also the key verse for the book of Acts. Where did the first century church get its power, the power to endure hardness as good soldiers of Jesus Christ, the power to go into all the world and preach the gospel to every creature, the power to suffer persecution even unto death? Where did they get their power?

The Bible says in Acts 4:33, *"And with great power gave the apostles witness of the resurrection of the Lord Jesus: and great grace was upon them all."* They did not simply witness of the resurrection of

Jesus Christ, they did it with great power. We know very little of this great power that was so evident in the first century church.

The Bible says in Hebrews 13:8, *"Jesus Christ the same yesterday, and to day, and for ever."* When we speak of our God, we speak of God the Father, God the Son, and God the Holy Spirit. Acts is the book of the continuing work of Christ in the Person of the Holy Spirit. Without the Lord Jesus Christ, we are lost and dead in our trespasses and sins. The power of God's Spirit quickens us from the dead and gives us life. The message preached in the first century church was the powerful message of the resurrected Savior, and it was proclaimed in the power of His resurrection.

In one verse of the New Testament we find the key to unlock the secret of the first century church. It is a matter of God's power.

God's Spirit indwells those who have been redeemed, who have asked God to forgive their sin, and by faith trusted in the finished work of Jesus Christ for salvation, who have been made alive by His Spirit. We have been redeemed by the precious blood of the Lamb. The Lord comes to abide in us forever. His desire is to empower us to do God's work God's way.

The Bible says in Matthew 28:18-20

> *And Jesus came and spake unto them, saying, All power is given unto me in heaven and in earth. Go ye therefore, and teach all nations, baptizing them in the name of the Father, and of the Son, and of the Holy Ghost: teaching them to observe all things whatsoever I have commanded you: and, lo, I am with you alway, even unto the end of the world. Amen.*

Notice the word *"power"* in verse eighteen. This is not the word *"power"* that is used for the dynamite, explosive power of God Paul speaks about in Romans 1:16 when he says, *"For I am not ashamed of the gospel of Christ: for it is the power of God unto salvation to every one that believeth; to the Jew first, and also to the Greek."*

This word *"power"* in Matthew 28 has to do with authority. The Lord Jesus Christ said that it is His right, His authority, to say what He is saying. He has all right, all power, all authority. It is all given to Him. Then He said, *"Go ye therefore, and teach all nations, baptizing them in the name of the Father, and of the Son, and of the Holy Ghost: teaching them to observe all things whatsoever I have commanded you."*

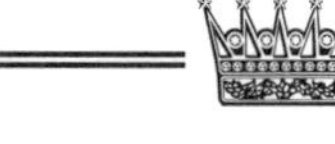

The message preached in the first century church was the powerful message of the resurrected Savior, and it was proclaimed in the power of His resurrection.

The Bible says in Luke 24:46-48,

> *And said unto them, Thus it is written, and thus it behoved Christ to suffer, and to rise from the dead the third day: and that repentance and remission of sins should be preached in his name among all nations, beginning at Jerusalem. And ye are witnesses of these things.*

We are witnesses. Jesus Christ said to His disciples, *"Ye are witnesses of these things."* Angels cannot preach the gospel. Angels cannot tell the story of salvation. They are not witnesses. But we who have been redeemed are witnesses.

In the matter of witnessing the *noun* must come before the *verb*. We are witnesses. We know what God has done in our lives. Because of this, we are able to witness to others. We must be a witness before we are able to witness.

The Lord Jesus said in Luke 24:49, *"And, behold, I send the promise of my Father upon you: but tarry ye in the city of Jerusalem, until ye be endued with power from on high."*

Notice the words *"until"* and *"power."* God told them not to attempt to do His work until they had His power. We must realize that we cannot do His work unless we have His power. If we attempt to do His work without His power, we will fail.

There is a disconnection or schism between God's work and God's people. Much confusion is brought on by ignorance of this principle in the Scripture.

If we attempt to do His work without His power, we will fail.

For example, most people have the idea that when we speak of the church we are speaking about a building where people meet. They confine all of their thoughts about the church to that meeting. The meeting of the church is just a meeting; it is not the church but the meeting of that church. We meet for the perfecting of the saints, so that they might do the work of the ministry. We meet for the edifying of the body of Christ, to have people built up in God's Word. But the great work of the church is done outside of the church building. Of course, the building can be used for many things as a meeting place for the local church work, but we are to do His work each day.

In other words, we need God's power, not just in the assembly, but we also need God's power as the church functions throughout the week. This means in order to do our jobs the right way as believers, in order to guide our homes, in order to instruct our children, in order to earn a living in a way that glorifies God, we must have God's power. Everything about our lives as Christians demands that we have God's power to accomplish His work in the way that God has designed to bring glory to Him.

We must not be confused when considering the power of the first century church. We are *not* simply speaking of having powerful meetings. These were people who were filled with God's power. They did not confine their faith to a building. We must not confine our faith to a building. If we do, we are all disconnected. In other words, a businessman should realize that he needs God's power just as the missionary needs God's power. He should understand that the reason he needs God's power is the same reason that the missionary needs God's power, so that each can do God's work. The two are working together, supporting each other. We are all in the Lord's work together. We are all depending on the same power, the power of God's Spirit to do God's work.

These were people who were filled with God's power. They did not confine their faith to a building.

Many times churches do not function God's way. In our attempts to substitute organizational structures and "how to" meetings for the power of God's Holy Spirit, the church becomes dysfunctional because we are attempting to accomplish God's work on the strength of our organization and not in the power of God's Holy Spirit. Our organization needs God's blessing and power but must never become a substitute for it.

So often when speaking with pastors about the Lord's work, I find that they are looking for some formula, some plan, some strategy. We have totally forgotten that there is a real Person, the Holy Spirit of God, who alone empowers us to do God's work.

Do you know Him? Is the personality of Jesus Christ being formed in your life by Him? Is the fruit of His Spirit evident in your life and mine?

Chapter Three

The power of the first century church was not about how they performed or what their strategy might have been. The power of the first century church rested entirely upon their dependence and allegiance to the Lord God, in the Person of His indwelling Holy Spirit. They were people of such prayer and dependence upon the Lord Jesus Christ.

We face so many temptations today in the Lord's work, and all of them translate into doing God's work in some way other than the way God has designed.

Physical Power

There are different powers in the world. There is obviously physical power. I have met people of brute strength who sometimes think because of their physical ability they can muscle their way through life without needing God.

Financial Power

There is a financial power. It is so sad to see people, even many Christian people, who think that the answer is to give more money to some thing. This happens often in world missions and evangelism. We think that the real answer is to raise more money and to give more to missionaries, believing that the more we raise, and the more we talk about money, the more we are going to get done for God. However, we could give untold millions to God's work and neglect the power of God's Holy Spirit, and God's work will never be accomplished.

Even in your home life, if you think that the answer is buying things and providing things for your family–a roof over their heads, clothes on their backs, a nice automobile in which to ride, an education–if you think that your need for power can be satisfied through financial means, then you have failed to understand what the first century church was all about.

Mental Power

Many people depend almost entirely on mental power. They think that the answer to everything is some sort of knowledge or education. There is no doubt that intellectual power or the ability to communicate ideas and to articulate thoughts well is a powerful tool, but it is a poor substitute for the power of God's Holy Spirit. This is especially evident when this happens in the training of ministers.

Are we moving, working, living, and breathing in the power of God's Holy Spirit? Are we functioning in the power of God's Holy Spirit? What does this mean? We learn from the Scripture that we are dead people. The Bible says in Ephesians 2:1, *"And you hath he quickened, who were dead in trespasses and sins."*

We also learn that when we are born into God's family, He quickens us from the dead. The Holy Spirit comes to live in us and gives us new birth, and we become the temple of God's Holy Spirit. Our bodies are His temple. The only real service that we can give God is the service of Christ in us. Everything accomplished without Jesus Christ is dead works. The only thing that God will be pleased with is Christ. He is the only perfect One. He is the only One who satisfies the righteousness and holiness of God.

The only One who truly pleases God the Father is God the Son. And the only work that we ever do for God, that pleases God, is when we die to self and allow God the Son, in the Person of the Holy Spirit to live through our lives.

Now if this be true, and I am convinced that it is, think how many things that we have done in life in our own energy, with our own mental capacity, with finances, or with physical ability that have not been done in the name of the Lord for the glory of the Lord. No wonder we have such impotence in churches and such emptiness in Christians. Let us yield ourselves to His control.

We have learned how to live without the power of God's Holy Spirit. What mother would say, "I cannot raise my children, or guide my children, I cannot prepare for the day or be guided through the day to do the right things unless I am dependent entirely upon God the Holy Spirit to guide and instruct me"?

We have learned how to live without the power of God's Holy Spirit.

What father would say, "The strength I must have to be a father, husband, and leader in my home is the power of God's Holy Spirit"? I dare say that ninety percent of the Christians I know associate God's Spirit and God's power with some meeting in a church house and are dislocated in their thinking about Him in their daily lives. Nothing could be further from the truth of the Bible.

Stop thinking of the power of the Holy Spirit in some mystical way. We are talking about a Person. We are simply stating that our lives need to be given to Him. We are to obey Him, trust Him, and abide in Him.

If I am going to live the Christian life, I need not forsake the assembling of myself with others. The Bible says in Hebrews 10:25, *"Not forsaking the assembling of ourselves together, as the manner of some is."* We need what we receive in the Spirit-filled church meeting, where the Bible is taught, God's Word is preached, and we sing great hymns that stir our hearts and teach Bible truth and doctrine. But if we are going to live the Christian life on a daily basis, we must come before God on a daily basis with the same attitude that we do in a church house, and say, "Lord, we need You."

I cannot be the husband that my wife deserves to have. I cannot be the father my children deserve to have, or the grandfather that my grandchildren deserve to have, or the friend my friends deserve to have without absolute dependence upon the Holy Spirit. Until we come to this persuasion of our absolute need of God, moment-by-moment, day-by-day, we are never going to have the power of the first century church.

The Lord Jesus Christ taught His disciples about the Holy Spirit. The Bible says in John 14:16-21,

> *And I will pray the Father, and he shall give you another Comforter, that he may abide with you for ever; even the Spirit of truth; whom the world cannot receive, because it seeth him not, neither knoweth him: but ye know him; for he dwelleth with you, and shall be in you. I will not leave you comfortless: I will come to you. Yet a little while, and the world seeth me no more; but ye see me: because I live, ye shall live also. At that day ye shall know that I am in my Father, and ye in me, and I in you. He that hath my commandments, and keepeth them, he it is that loveth me: and he that loveth me shall be loved of my Father, and I will love him, and will manifest myself to him.*

Our Lord said in John 14:26,

> *But the Comforter, which is the Holy Ghost, whom the Father will send in my name, he shall teach you all things, and bring all things to your remembrance, whatsoever I have said unto you.*

Notice what the Lord Jesus said concerning the Holy Spirit in John 16:7-15,

> *Nevertheless I tell you the truth; It is expedient for you that I go away: for if I go not away, the Comforter will not come unto you; but if I depart, I will send him unto you. And when he is come, he will reprove the world of sin, and of righteousness, and of judgment: of*

sin, because they believe not on me; of righteousness, because I go to my Father, and ye see me no more; of judgment, because the prince of this world is judged. I have yet many things to say unto you, but ye cannot bear them now. Howbeit when he, the Spirit of truth, is come, he will guide you into all truth: for he shall not speak of himself; but whatsoever he shall hear, that shall he speak: and he will shew you things to come. He shall glorify me: for he shall receive of mine, and shall shew it unto you. All things that the Father hath are mine: therefore said I, that he shall take of mine, and shall shew it unto you.

The spirit of fear in our lives is evidence that we are not living consciously in the power of God's Holy Spirit.

What about our dependence upon God the Holy Spirit? The Bible says in Acts 1:8, *"But ye shall receive power, after that the Holy Ghost is come upon you: and ye shall be witnesses unto me both in Jerusalem, and in all Judaea, and in Samaria, and unto the uttermost part of the earth."*

I think that this statement startled the disciples. He looked at this small group, small compared to the task of world evangelism, and He said to them, *"But ye shall receive power, after that the Holy Ghost is come upon you: and ye shall be witnesses unto me both in Jerusalem, and in all Judaea, and in Samaria, and unto the uttermost part of the earth."*

If you talk about being a witness in Jerusalem, and Judea, and Samaria, and unto the uttermost part of the earth and leave God out, it is an impossible task. This startled them to the point that they were awakened. Their senses were moved. They thought, "How can it be?" Then they realized from what He was talking about that it could only be done in the power of the Holy Spirit. They knew from what He said in Luke 24 that they must pray and wait upon God until they be endued with this power from on high.

The Bible says in Acts 2:1-3,

> *And when the day of Pentecost was fully come, they were all with one accord in one place. And suddenly there came a sound from heaven as of a rushing mighty wind, and it filled all the house where they were sitting. And there appeared unto them cloven tongues like as of fire, and it sat upon each of them.*

The Holy Spirit came that day to take over, to rule, to have authority, to take control.

The Bible says in Acts 2:4-6,

> *And they were all filled with the Holy Ghost, and began to speak with other tongues, as the Spirit gave them utterance. And there were dwelling at Jerusalem Jews, devout men, out of every nation under heaven. Now when this was noised abroad, the multitude came together, and were confounded, because that every man heard them speak in his own language.*

The Holy Spirit filled these apostles, and they were able to speak in known languages that the people understood. The people understood the gospel, the message of Jesus Christ in their own language. This was the work of the Spirit of God. Can you imagine what a magnificent, miraculous thing was taking place there? As they were praying, the Holy Spirit came and took control. As they were praying and waiting on God, the Holy Spirit came and filled them with power. (This would be a great time to go back to the introduction in this book and read again what C.H. Spurgeon said about miracles.)

Chapter Three

The Bible says in Acts 2:14, *"But Peter, standing up with the eleven, lifted up his voice, and said unto them, Ye men of Judaea, and all ye that dwell at Jerusalem, be this known unto you, and hearken to my words."* It was the Spirit of God that gave Peter this sermon. They were experiencing this power God promised.

The Bible says in Acts 2:41, *"Then they that gladly received his word were baptized: and the same day there were added unto them about three thousand souls."*

Think of churches across our land that are weak and anemic, timid and fearful... What is missing? We leave God out completely.

In other words, God had so anointed and filled Peter with His Spirit, that when Peter preached, three thousand people were saved. They saw first-hand the power of the first century church.

The Bible says in Acts 6:8, *"And Stephen, full of faith and power, did great wonders and miracles among the people."* God gave grace to the faithful deacon Stephen. It cost him his life. How could a man bear up under this? He could only do this with the power of God's Holy Spirit.

The Bible says in Acts 8:5, *"Then Philip went down to the city of Samaria, and preached Christ unto them."* God by His Spirit led a man to do something out of the ordinary and took him in a certain direction. How did Philip know this was what he was supposed to do? He was being guided by the Holy Spirit. He knew the Lord and the Person of God's Holy Spirit. He experienced the power of the first century church as God guided him.

The Bible says in Acts 10:1-6,

> *There was a certain man in Caesarea called Cornelius, a centurion of the band called the Italian*

> *band, a devout man, and one that feared God with all his house, which gave much alms to the people, and prayed to God alway. He saw in a vision evidently about the ninth hour of the day an angel of God coming in to him, and saying unto him, Cornelius. And when he looked on him, he was afraid, and said, What is it, Lord? And he said unto him, Thy prayers and thine alms are come up for a memorial before God. And now send men to Joppa, and call for one Simon, whose surname is Peter: he lodgeth with one Simon a tanner, whose house is by the sea side: he shall tell thee what thou oughtest to do.*

Cornelius was to learn of the mighty work of the Holy Spirit. There was someone involved in this other than Cornelius. There was someone involved in this other than Peter. There was an invasion by God's Holy Spirit in the lives of Cornelius and Peter. God by His Spirit directed Peter. Through the vision, Peter saw God direct him in this powerful way that as a Jew he was to go preach the gospel to the Gentile Cornelius.

Are you living day-by-day in such a way that you personally witness the power of God's Holy Spirit demonstrated in your life? Is it possible?

The Bible says in II Timothy 1:7, *"For God hath not given us the spirit of fear; but of power, and of love, and of a sound mind."* Most people I know are not living a powerful life. They are living with the spirit of fear, timid, frightened, and afraid to move forward, afraid to attempt anything for God. When the least thing goes wrong with their children, they worry and fret. When the least thing goes wrong in the home, things begin to unravel. When the least thing happens in their marriage, they become frightened. When the least thing comes physically that touches their body and gets their attention, they become nervous and upset. We are all guilty of this. The spirit of fear in our lives is evidence that we are not living consciously in the power of God's Holy Spirit.

Think of churches across our land that are weak and anemic, timid and fearful. To compound the situation, many of them have timid, weak, fearful pastors, and lay people serving as deacons and Sunday School teachers and women working in the church who are timid and fearful. What is missing? In our attempts to organize and to function, in our attempts to get some committee doing something to establish a plan, in our attempts to strategize and to consider all our resources, we forget God. We leave God out completely. As I stated earlier, we are disconnected from God the Holy Spirit. We are dysfunctional in the way the church should function, and we call that dysfunction, function. The flesh is so pleased, and so proud of it. We substitute men's measure of success for what could be done in the power of God's Holy Spirit. We get results, but they are the meager, anemic results that our energy and our flesh can produce. And we sit empty, not knowing, never discovering, never realizing, and never experiencing what God by His mighty power can accomplish in and through our lives in our churches. O may God help us! May there be a hungering and a thirsting for the power of the first century church.

We substitute men's measure of success for what could be done in the power of God's Holy Spirit. We get results, but they are the meager, anemic results that our energy and our flesh can produce.

When the expression "the first century church" is used, please do not confine it to a meeting, to some place where you say the preacher preached a great sermon, and the singing was wonderful and honored the Lord. Please do not make that terrible mistake.

When we are talking about the power of the first century church, we are talking about people who lived separated lives, separated unto God and from the world, those who lived victoriously over sin, who took their burdens to the Lord. When unforeseen circumstances came to them, they realized they had a God who made the world, who lived in them, and they were not frightened and fearful. They knew that God would see them through.

We need the dynamic of that Spirit-filled life that testified to a true and living God. As you look through your Bible, especially the book of Acts, you see some obvious things. You see that this power, the Holy Spirit, who is a Person, who develops Jesus Christ in us, changed these people. We see that the Holy Spirit changed these lives in many ways.

He Changed Their Speech

There is no doubt that these humble fishermen were men who could talk. One could hear them sometimes on the Sea of Galilee, their voices roaring and laughter filling the air. They could speak, but when they came to a personal encounter with God the Holy Spirit, and He filled them, their speech changed. Their speech now was about the Lord Jesus Christ and was used to bring glory to Him.

I get deeply concerned about some professing Christian men and women who are never talking about the Lord Jesus. They would rather talk about an athletic event than talk about Jesus Christ. They would rather talk about personal achievements than talk about the Lord Jesus Christ.

One of the indicators that reminds me I am not what I should be as a Christian is when I start talking about what I have done and what I have accomplished. I recognize that I have lost contact with God. The self-promoting life is not evidence of a Spirit-filled life.

What about your conversation? When something goes wrong, and you have to deal with it, if you blow up about the thing, that is evidence that you are not in communion with Jesus Christ as you should be. If you were really in communion with Christ as you should be, you could handle these things because you would be living consciously in the presence of God the Holy Spirit, and God the Holy Spirit can deal with all things. Our speech would be different. He changes the way we speak.

My wife and I want to experience a certain intimacy in our marriage in the way we treat one another. To me there is nothing as sweet on earth as that. I am not even talking about the physical side of it, which is a wonderful gift God gives to marriage, but just the way we treat one another. The truth is, when she is the Christian she should be, and I am the Christian I should be, when we are abiding in the Lord as we should abide in the Lord Jesus, we treat one another the way we should treat one another. It changes, not only what we say, but also the tone that we use when speaking to one another. It is the power of God's Holy Spirit that changes the way we speak.

He Gave Them Courage

The Bible says in Acts 4:13, *"Now when they saw the boldness of Peter and John, and perceived that they were unlearned and ignorant men, they marvelled; and they took knowledge of them, that they had been with Jesus."* Many times when people read this verse and comment on it, they emphasize the fact that these unlearned and ignorant men were bold. But the point is that the accusers witnessed courage in these men that they could not explain, and they concluded that it was obviously not a result of their education or training.

The religious leaders said, "We are learned men. We are doctors of the law. We have a great understanding of the things of God and the Scripture, and yet they speak to us with courage and boldness. Where does this courage and boldness come from? These are unlearned and ignorant men." You and I know where the boldness came from; they received it from the Spirit of God.

When we are ashamed to give a gospel tract, when we are ashamed to witness, ashamed to speak His name, cowardly about our faith, that is a great indication for us that we have not given God the Holy Spirit the place in our lives that He is to have. He changes people.

He Gave Them Vision

Study the prejudices of Jewish people, the way they confined God to themselves. Their attitude was, "This is the God of the Hebrews. This is the God of the Jews. He is Jehovah God, the covenant God of Israel." But something happened to them when they were filled with the Holy Spirit; they got a vision for all people. They wanted everyone to know Christ. They realized they were to go *"into all the world"* and preach Jesus Christ.

I do not know how many times we have to go through this before we will ever learn. People need the Lord. There are people everywhere groping in darkness and moving rapidly toward a Devil's hell. The truth is, when we are filled with God's Spirit, when we truly know something of the power of the first century church, our vision will be so enlarged that we will see that all people need the gospel. By our yielding to God, we receive His vision of a lost world.

The Christian life is so much simpler than most have ever made it. If I am living the life that God has designed for me to live, then the Lord has His rightful place in my life. I will be a hopeful person, helpful, encouraging others. I will know that greater is He that is in me than he that is in the world.

IV

The Authority of the First Century Church

e are living in perilous times, in an increasingly unhappy world. The farther people move from God and God's Word, the more miserable they are going to become. Their misery is veiled by *"the pleasures of sin for a season."*

People are trying every vanity in this world to gain happiness, plunging in again and again and coming up empty, *"ever learning and never able to come to the knowledge of the truth."* There is no true fulfillment outside of knowing Jesus Christ and living a life of obedience to Him.

The Bible says in II Timothy 3:13-17,

> *But evil men and seducers shall wax worse and worse, deceiving, and being deceived. But continue thou in the things which thou hast learned and hast been assured of, knowing of whom thou hast learned them; and that from a child thou hast known the*

> *holy scriptures, which are able to make thee wise unto salvation through faith which is in Christ Jesus. All scripture is given by inspiration of God, and is profitable for doctrine, for reproof, for correction, for instruction in righteousness: that the man of God may be perfect, throughly furnished unto all good works.*

The term *"holy scriptures"* is used in reference to the Bible. The word *"scriptures"* means "writings." These are not just writings; these are the holy writings of God. When we hold the Bible in our hands, we are holding the *"holy scriptures."*

The Bible is God's written revelation of Himself to man. It is a Book about God.

The Bible is God's written revelation of Himself to man. It is a Book about God. It is progressive in its revelation. Our Lord is perfectly revealed in the Person of His Son, the Lord Jesus Christ. The Lord Jesus said in John 14:9, *"He that hath seen me hath seen the Father."*

We find an amazing truth about these holy Scriptures in Psalm 119:89. The Bible says, *"For ever, O LORD, thy word is settled in heaven."* Before any word of the Bible was ever given to men to pen, every word of the Bible was settled in heaven forever. When God says forever, that is what He means. *"For ever, O LORD, thy word is settled in heaven."*

In Psalm 119:152 the Bible says, *"Concerning thy testimonies, I have known of old that thou hast founded them for ever."* We are able to hold in our hands and hide in our hearts the only eternal thing the human eye will ever look upon.

In II Timothy chapter three, God's Word deals with the subject of *"perilous times."* The chapter begins, *"This know also, that in the last days perilous times shall come."* Then a list is given in verses two through five of things that characterize these perilous times.

> *For men shall be lovers of their own selves, covetous, boasters, proud, blasphemers, disobedient to parents, unthankful, unholy, without natural affection, trucebreakers, false accusers, incontinent, fierce, despisers of those that are good, traitors, heady, highminded, lovers of pleasures more than lovers of God; having a form of godliness, but denying the power thereof: from such turn away.*

What a list! Paul says, *"Having a form of godliness."* The most dangerous error is the error that attempts to disguise itself in the garments of religion. These risky or perilous times bring to the forefront *"a form of godliness"* that is not of God.

Have all these things existed in every civilization? Certainly they have, but they are completely characteristic of our age. They have been woven into the fabric of our times. Worldwide these things characterize our day.

On the list is the word *"incontinent."* This word means "falling apart; being torn apart; coming apart." We are living in a world that is literally breaking apart.

It is impossible to be spiritual without being scriptural.

The word *"fierce"* means "savagely violent." Many are filled with fear. The Bible says the terrible thing about all of this is that *"evil men and seducers shall wax worse and worse."* But we are not to bury our heads in the sand.

We have an understanding of the times in which we live. We are not to be frightened because *"God hath not given us the spirit of fear; but of power, and of love, and of a sound mind"* (II Timothy 1:7).

So what are we to do? We are to do exactly what we find in the Bible. God takes us directly to His Word. In these perilous times, He brings us to the holy Scriptures.

The Bible says for us to continue in the things we have been assured of, *"But continue thou in the things which thou hast learned and hast been assured of, knowing of whom thou hast learned them; and that from a child thou hast known the holy scriptures."* There is a work that only the Word of God can accomplish.

I can remember when I received my first Bible. When I was nine years old, while visiting the doctor, I received an invitation to go to Sunday School. The pediatrician happened to be a Sunday School teacher, and he invited my mother to bring me to his class. My mother made sure I got there. When I got to his class, he gave me a little Bible. I still have that Bible.

I knew that Bible was important, and I knew that it was a precious Book when I received it. But with every passing year, I realize more and more how precious the Bible truly is. It is an anchor for our souls. It is God's fixed point of reference in a world that is always changing. To our shame, there is nothing in human life so valuable yet so neglected as the Bible. It is available to us, but we do not make ourselves available to God's Word.

Everything we see around us should be judged through scriptural eyes, meaning that we should not look at the world to interpret the Bible; we should search the Scriptures to interpret what is going on in the world. It is impossible to be spiritual without being scriptural. Let us determine to live by the clear teaching of the Bible.

The Inspiration of All Scripture

When attempting to speak the truth, it is always better to use the very language of the Bible if at all possible. Fix in your mind the language of the Bible. *"All scripture is given by inspiration of God."* Many say the Bible is inspired in spots, and they happen to be inspired to tell us which spots. Let there be no confusion in the vital matter–*"All scripture is given by inspiration of God."*

Often when people are talking about the Bible and the human instrumentality God used to pen the Bible, they speak of the writers being inspired. The inspiration of Scripture is not referring to the inspiration of the writers, but to the writings. God revealed His words to men.

There are those who tell us that it was the thoughts that God inspired, leaving the writers of Scripture free to clothe those thoughts in their own words. This can lead easily to the statement that the Bible contains the Word of God. The amazing thing about this is that it is exactly the reverse of the truth.

If we believe the testimony of the Scripture, we must say that God always gave the words but did not always reveal to them the thoughts. This is made perfectly clear by certain passages of Scripture.

For example, in I Peter 1:10-11 the Bible says,

> *Of which salvation the prophets have inquired and searched diligently, who prophesied of the grace that should come unto you: searching what, or what manner of time the Spirit of Christ which was in them did signify, when it testified beforehand the sufferings of Christ, and the glory that should follow.*

In this passage we see that when the prophets wrote of Christ, they actually had to study the prophecies they themselves had written, and even then they did not fully understand what they had written.

In Daniel 12:8-9 the Bible says, *"And I heard but I understood not, then said I, O my Lord, what shall be the end of these things?*

And he said, Go thy way, Daniel: for the words are closed up and sealed to the time of the end."

Here we find Daniel writing words given to him by divine inspiration which Daniel himself could not understand. He had to think about what he had written. Though God gave him the very words to write, he *"understood not."*

The spade of the archeologist has never unearthed anything that has disproved the inspiration of Scripture. The Scriptures themselves testify to divine inspiration, and of course the testimony of the Lord Jesus Christ gives witness to the inspiration of Scripture. *"All scripture is given by inspiration of God."*

The spade of the archeologist has never unearthed anything that has disproved the inspiration of Scripture.

The Bible is a true record because it is God-breathed and God cannot lie. For example, when the Devil gives directives, do not listen to him; he is a liar. He told Eve she would not die—he lied. Though the Bible records this statement given by Satan which is not the truth, it is a true record of the statement made by the Devil. We must know who is speaking and to whom God's Word is speaking, because everything in the Bible is a true record. It is God's Word.

Taking verses out of context has caused grave errors, and if one does that, he can prove almost anything he desires to prove. I can tell you that it is right to go out and hang yourself if I take out of context the story of Judas Iscariot hanging himself. No, the Bible does not say to go out and hang yourself. But God gives us a true record of what Judas Iscariot did. After he betrayed Christ, he went out and hanged himself.

The entire Bible is God-breathed. Consider the words of Jesus Christ in Matthew 4:4. When our Lord was being tempted of the

Devil, He defeated the Devil with the Word of God. The Bible says, *"But he answered and said, It is written, Man shall not live by bread alone, but by every word that proceedeth out of the mouth of God."* This is a wonderful description given by our Savior of inspiration, every word proceeding out of the mouth of God.

God only wrote one Book. As you hold the Bible in your hand, you have the one Book God wrote. Can you imagine that the Creator God who made you and spoke the world into existence, our all-wise God, our Almighty God, the God before whom we shall stand some day, has written a Book? Every word of that Book was settled before any word of it was ever given to men to pen. Every word of it came from the very mouth of God.

May God illuminate our minds and teach us the doctrine of inspiration. *"All scripture is given by inspiration of God."*

The Necessity of All Scripture

Let us place emphasis on all Scripture. This is a neglected truth. The Bible says in II Timothy 3:16, *"All scripture is given by inspiration of God."*

When speaking of the necessity of Scripture, we get the idea that we are dealing with Scripture in general. But if we emphasize the necessity of all Scripture, we must also consider the Scriptures specifically. By specifically I mean every Scripture. By this we are referring to every book of the Bible and every chapter in every book of the Bible. Most Christians are only familiar with parts of the Bible. They may be extremely familiar with certain parts of the Bible, but very few Christians are familiar with *"all scripture."*

In a puzzle, all pieces are necessary to complete the whole. The puzzle is incomplete if any piece is missing—it may even be a very small piece. The Bible is God's revelation of Himself to us.

Chapter Four

The Bible is a Book of sixty-six books. Each book is necessary to complete the whole. Each book has a specific message that is a part of the big picture of the entire Book.

It is our Lord's desire to complete His children. Each message from each book is necessary to accomplish this goal. No book can be overlooked. If the message of one book is neglected in our lives, we cannot have all God has for us. If you took one book out of the Bible, it would not be complete. If you took Obadiah out or Joel out or Habakkuk or Philemon out, the Bible would not be complete.

When God breathed these words for men to pen, He gave every book for a purpose. In every book of the Bible, God has a specific message for His children concerning Himself.

When God breathed these words for men to pen, He gave every book for a purpose. In every book of the Bible, God has a specific message for His children concerning Himself. The sixty-six books are all necessary to complete the message of God to men.

What has the book of Joel revealed to us about God? What has the book of Obadiah told us of God? What has God said to you through the book of Habakkuk? What has God said to you through the book of Leviticus? What has God said to you through the book of Jude? What has God said to you through the book of Romans? What has God said to you through the book of Judges? What has God said to you through the book of Lamentations? Immediately all of us are quite ashamed because we are not familiar with some of these books of the Bible. Remember that each book reveals something to us concerning our God.

God did not give us one Book; He gave us sixty-six books in this one Book because the message of each book is necessary. If you remove the message of any one of the books, then there is something incomplete about all that God wants us to know concerning Himself. Every one of God's children should read the Bible, search the Scriptures, meditate on the Scriptures, memorize Scriptures, and ask God by His Spirit to teach him the message of each book of the Bible. Most Christians are traveling through this world spending very little time with the message God has for each of us.

If we really agree concerning the necessity of all Scripture, then we should not be neglecting any Scripture. Our lives are incomplete without God's message from each book of the Bible.

Imagine the certain pieces of clothing that are worn to get dressed. It takes every piece of clothing to be properly attired. If I take a piece of that clothing out of my daily wardrobe, then I am not properly attired; something is missing.

When God gave us sixty-six books of the Bible, He gave us each book to help us be the children of God He desires for us to be. Without having all these books of the Bible and the message of each of these books, we miss much of what God has for us. Often we speak of the "balanced" life. Let us change the word to *complete*—complete in Christ. God uses all His Word to make us complete in Him. The Holy Scriptures are all inspired and all necessary.

The Sufficiency of All Scripture

We know that Christ is all-sufficient. The Bible tells us our sufficiency is of God. *"For in him dwelleth all the fulness of the Godhead bodily"* (Colossians 2:9). He is enough; He is everything we need. We should not say that we believe in the all-sufficient Savior without saying we believe in the all-sufficient Scriptures.

God has told us from His Word that He knows what is in man (John 2:25). I do not know about men by studying men; I know about men by knowing God. He created men.

If you have a problem with your children, you do not need to know more about your children; you need to know more of God who made your children and gave them to you. He will reveal to you how you are to deal with your children. He teaches us through His all-sufficient Word.

> *Look no farther than God's Word for a manual for the Christian life.*

The Bible declares that we are to live with our wives *"according to knowledge"* (I Peter 3:7). We are to know them. How can we know them? If we know God better, God will teach us. He made our wives. He will teach us how we are to love them and treat them. He knows what is in them.

Declaring that the Scriptures are all-sufficient is declaring that God's Word meets every need. Go to God's Word with your needs.

The Lord gives us insight in II Timothy 3:15, *"And that from a child thou hast known the holy scriptures, which are able to make thee wise unto salvation."* The greatest need we have is salvation, and God says the first thing His Word does is make us *"wise unto salvation."* We must know how to have our sins forgiven, and the holy Scriptures give us the answer by making us *"wise unto salvation."*

The Bible goes on to say, *"All scripture is given by inspiration of God, and is profitable for doctrine." "Doctrine"* is what we believe and teach. We find in the Bible what we are to believe about everything–about life and death, heaven and hell, angels, things to come, immorality and decency and such issues as homosexuality. Our philosophy for life should come out of the right theology, our knowledge of God from His Word.

The Bible is given to us for *"reproof."* This means to point out to us where we are wrong. No one likes to hear he is wrong, but the Bible is truth, and truth reveals error. There is no telling how far we could drift if we did not have the Bible to reprove us.

The Bible says God's Word is given to us for *"correction."* This is to show us what is right.

Then the Word of God says, *"for instruction in righteousness."* The Holy Spirit applies the Bible to our lives. He patiently stays with us until we are doing what is right.

"That the man of God may be perfect." In this context, the Lord is not speaking only of a preacher; but of every Christian. The word *"perfect"* means "complete." Everything we need to complete our lives is given to us in Scripture. Remember our thoughts concerning the necessity of all Scripture. Do not run first to some book on your shelf. Of course, many books are helpful. I have written many that I hope are helpful. But go first *to* God's Word and do not go *from* God's Word.

Declaring that the Scriptures are all-sufficient is declaring that God's Word meets every need.

"...Throughly furnished unto all good works." Everything we need to equip us to be the laborers we must be, we get from the Bible. Look no farther than God's Word for a manual for the Christian life.

Because of what we believe to be true concerning God's Word, we should seek as much as possible to use the very language of Scripture when speaking of the things of God.

- God's words are more powerful than man's words.
- God's words have more authority than man's words.
- God's words are clearer than man's words.

- God's words are more convicting than man's words.
- God's words provide a safeguard for Bible doctrine better than man's words.
- God's words are more complete than man's words.

In the work of the Lord, men most often use the language of the world. Those who have the responsibility of teaching and preaching the Bible should use the language of the Bible as much as possible. Men use the word *alcoholic*; God's Word uses the word *"drunkard"* (Proverbs 23:21). In the words of men, we hear of the balanced life; God's Word speaks of being "complete in Christ" (Colossians 2:10). As a substitute for faith, we often hear people speaking of "keeping your focus"; the Word of God says, *"looking unto Jesus"* (Hebrews 12:2). Does it have more authority, is it more powerful, is it clearer, is it more convicting, to tell people to stay focused or to "look unto Jesus" and keep their eyes on Christ?

Baptists are fond of using the expression, "Once saved; always saved." This expression is dangerous because it gives people the idea they can make a profession of faith and then live any way they please. God's Word does not speak of being "once saved; always saved," but rather of possessing *"eternal life"* (John 10:28). Again, many Christian leaders speak of those who have compromised the faith. According to God's Word, it is not a matter of compromise, but of obeying or disobeying our Lord's clear commands.

Our attitude toward God's Word is our attitude toward God. The first century church was a church wholly dependent upon God and His Word. To become a first century church, we must have a revolution back to the Bible.

V

The Doctrine of the First Century Church

It is not our work to build the church. Though there are some men who are used in the destruction of local churches, it is the Lord who builds the church as we obey Him.

It is our work to obey the Lord, and it is His work to give the increase. Our work is entirely the work of obedience! We need to know the Bible and to obey what God has told us to do. We understand the clear commands of God so that we might be obedient to those commands. The Bible is not a book of suggestions but a book of clear commands.

The Lord Jesus said, *"I will build my church"* (Matthew 16:18). Remember, He did not say, "I will build *your* church"; He did not say, "You will build *my* church." He said, *"I will build my church."* I sincerely desire to be the pastor that God would have me to be and that our people deserve to have.

The Bible says in Acts 2:41-42,

> *Then they that gladly received his word were baptized: and the same day there were added unto them about three thousand souls. And they continued stedfastly in the apostles' doctrine and fellowship, and in breaking of bread, and in prayers.*

The Bible says that they continued steadfastly in the *"apostles' doctrine."* The apostles were men chosen of the Lord. They were men who were eyewitnesses of the resurrected Christ. They were men who received their message directly from God. The Bible says that they preached God's Word, and people came to Christ. People heard the truth, received the Lord Jesus as their Savior, and continued in the apostles' doctrine.

It is our work to obey the Lord, and it is His work to give the increase.

We are dealing with the doctrine of the first century church. Is it possible that after all these centuries we can still have the same doctrine that the first century church had? Yes! Absolutely.

God's Word liveth and abideth forever, and the sole authority for our faith and practice is the Word of God. We can know the doctrine of the first century church, and we can continue in that doctrine in this present hour.

On one of my visits to the Metropolitan Tabernacle in London, the issue of Bible doctrine was brought powerfully to my attention. My interest in Spurgeon aroused so many questions in my mind. So I went to one of the staff members there and I said, "I would like to see anything here that is related directly to the ministry of Charles Spurgeon. I know the portico and the columns out front are the same as they were then, but is there anything else that is exactly the same as it was when Spurgeon was here?"

The man said, "No, there is nothing else like that to see." I just knew somehow that he could find something for me to see, and so I said again with great earnestness, "Sir, is there anything here that is exactly the way it was when Charles Spurgeon was the pastor?" He looked me squarely in the eyes and said, "Yes, our doctrine. We still believe and teach the same thing."

There are churches that have come to grips with the doctrine of the first century church, and they have continued through the centuries with that body of doctrine in belief and principle. When you examine what you believe and teach, can you trace every bit of it to the first century church?

> *Is it possible that after all these centuries we can still have the same doctrine that the first century church had? Yes! Absolutely.*

Think seriously of our responsibility. I Timothy 3:15 says, *"But if I tarry long, that thou mayest know how thou oughtest to behave thyself in the house of God, which is the church of the living God, the pillar and ground of the truth."*

God tells us that we have a mighty responsibility. As a matter of fact, we are singularly held accountable with the responsibility of being the pillar and ground of the truth. The only thing that you can pass from one generation to the next in God's work is truth, not experience.

The Bible teaches that we worship God in spirit and in truth. We must worship God in truth. Truth is expressed in words. As much as possible, we should express the truth of God in the very words of Scripture.

Chapter Five

II Timothy 3:10-11 says,

> *But thou hast fully known my doctrine, manner of life, purpose, faith, longsuffering, charity, patience, persecutions, afflictions, which came unto me at Antioch, at Iconium, at Lystra; what persecutions I endured: but out of them all the Lord delivered me.*

Notice at the top of Paul's list when he writes to Timothy, he says, *"Thou hast fully known my doctrine."* The word *"doctrine"* means our teaching. The Lord Jesus left the church two things. He left us what we call *doctrine*, and He left us *ordinances*. The ordinances, which are baptism and the Lord's Supper, are the things that He *ordered* that we do. Both of them picture His death.

> *The only thing that you can pass from one generation to the next in God's work is truth, not experience.*

When someone obeys Christ in baptism, as he stands in the water, the water crosses his body like the cross where Christ died. He goes beneath the water as our Lord went into the grave, and he comes up out of the water as our Lord came out of the grave.

We must have the right candidate for baptism, which is a saved person. We must have the right mode, which is immersion, because it is the only mode of baptism that pictures the death, burial, and resurrection of Jesus Christ. And we must have the right authority for baptism. It is not a ministerial ordinance; it is a local church ordinance. The Lord Jesus gave this ordinance to the local church.

When we see someone baptized, it tells us again that Christ died for us, He was buried for us, and He rose from the dead for us. It pictures our death with Him, our burial with Him, and the new life that we have in Him. It identifies us with the Lord Jesus Christ and with that local assembly of baptized believers.

In the Lord's Supper, we have the juice and the bread. They picture His blood that was shed for us and His body that was broken for us. Christ left us these ordinances.

Then He also left us doctrine. This is our belief and teaching. Paul let us know that he had spent enough time teaching Timothy, so that he fully knew his doctrine. He had already told Timothy that he must find faithful men and commit to those faithful men what had already been committed to him. Those faithful men would teach it to others!

I hope you understand that through the centuries, there have been people who have vigilantly guarded the truth of God's Word, who would not budge or bend and paid for it with their own blood! They were able to give the next generation the same truth that they had received. This is a vital matter!

The Bible says in II Timothy 3:16, *"All scripture is given by inspiration of God, and is profitable for doctrine."* We get our doctrine from the Bible. Our teaching comes from the Bible. These are not man-made commands; these are truths that we find from the Bible!

II Timothy 4:1-4 says,

> *I charge thee therefore before God, and the Lord Jesus Christ, who shall judge the quick and the dead at his appearing and his kingdom; preach the word; be instant in season, out of season; reprove, rebuke, exhort with all longsuffering and doctrine. For the time will come when they will not endure sound doctrine; but after their own lusts shall they heap to themselves teachers, having itching ears; and they shall turn away their ears from the truth, and shall be turned unto fables.*

Chapter Five

We have been warned, *"The time will come when they will not endure sound doctrine."* Many have de-emphasized doctrine. They use cute expressions, such as, "Doctrine is not really important; it is our love and fellowship that is important! What is important is that we tolerate anything and everything in the name of love and tolerance. We do not make much of doctrine, because doctrine divides."

If we are obedient to God, God will teach us the truth of His Word.

Anything we attempt to build that is not built on truth is not of God. We need to make much of doctrine. We pass from our lives to the lives of those who are following us the truth of God's Word. It is Bible doctrine. We must keep the sacred trust that has been committed to us! Our faith is a *treasured heritage*, not a *contemporary experiment.*

Christ Has Given Us A Body of Doctrine

Our doctrine came from God. The Bible says in Acts 2:1, *"And they continued stedfastly in the apostles' doctrine."*

This office of an apostle no longer exists. The work of the apostle, meaning being a "sent one," still exists. But as far as being a person who has seen the resurrected Christ and received doctrine from God directly, and a person chosen by the Lord Jesus, we no longer meet those qualifications. If someone tells you that he has seen Christ, he did not see Christ as the apostles saw Him.

The Lord gave the apostles His doctrine. They taught it to others, and those they taught, taught it to others. The Bible says clearly that they continued in the apostles' doctrine. They made very sure that they got this teaching correct.

Remember what our Lord said of His doctrine. John 7:16-17 says, *"Jesus answered them, and said, My doctrine is not mine, but his that sent me. If any man will do his will, he shall know of the doctrine, whether it be of God, or whether I speak of myself."*

The amazing thing that is overlooked in this verse is that we can know this doctrine. If we are obedient to God, God will teach us the truth of His Word. The Bible is the written revelation of God. God revealed His Word to men who were moved along by the Spirit of God.

We must keep the sacred trust that has been committed to us! Our faith is a treasured heritage, *not a* contemporary experiment.

We have the inspired Scriptures, the writings of God. The Bible says of itself, it *"liveth and abideth for ever"* (I Peter 1:23). Every word of it is *"settled in heaven"* (Psalm 119:89). We have the Word of God and we can know God's Word!

The Bible says, *"If any man will do his will."* Are you willing to do His will? Some of you cannot know what God wants you to know because at some point you have stopped short in your obedience to Him. If you think that it is a light matter that you do not obey God in the simple, clear, and plain commands that He gives us, you are wrong!

Christ gave us this body of doctrine! He put it in the hands and hearts of those who loved Him and followed Him! He gave it to His disciples. His disciples gave it to others. They in turn gave it to others, and finally, winding through the centuries, someone gave it to us. This is absolutely essential. It is vital that we do not change it. We must give it to others just the way that God gave it to us.

Corrupting Influences Are Always at Work

Satan seeks to corrupt the truth by adding to it or by presenting only part of it. Seventeen times in the New Testament, the word *"leaven"* is used. In my understanding of Scripture, every time it is used, it implies something evil.

Take note of this parable the Lord Jesus gave in one verse. Matthew 13:33 says, *"Another parable spake he unto them; The kingdom of heaven is like unto leaven, which a woman took, and hid in three measures of meal, till the whole was leavened."*

The woman engaged in a deceptive deed. She hid the leaven. There are people who interpret this parable wrongly. They have the idea that the leaven is a good thing. Finally, the leaven leavens the whole lump. Everything is affected by it. But that is not good. If the leaven is something that is evil, then it should not be in the meal to leaven the whole lump and to make it all corrupt.

The Lord Jesus warned about leaven. Take note of those warnings. The Devil is always attempting to corrupt. It is not that he denies the truth as much as he adds to it.

The Lord mentioned three types of leaven during His ministry. In Matthew 16:6 the Bible says, *"Then Jesus said unto them, Take heed and beware of the leaven of the Pharisees and of the Sadducees."*

What is the leaven of the Pharisees? In Luke 12:1 the Bible declares, *"In the mean time, when there were gathered together an innumerable multitude of people, insomuch that they trode one upon another, he began to say unto his disciples first of all, Beware ye of the leaven of the Pharisees, which is hypocrisy."*

The leaven of the Pharisees was hypocrisy. The Pharisees were the religious leaders of the day. The Lord Jesus warned that their leaven was hypocrisy. They were not who they appeared to be. They were wearing masks.

There are people who disguise themselves as preachers, and there are places that disguise themselves as churches, and they tell people things that are not in God's Word. They do not line up with the Bible.

Take heed. You cannot be moved simply by emotion; by the afflictions of others and the hard times they have gone through. Remember what Paul wrote to Timothy, reminding him, *"Thou hast fully known my doctrine..."* Then after that he said, *"...manner of life,"* and then *"...persecutions and afflictions."* He did not start with persecutions and afflictions. He began with doctrine. Are we hearing the truth?

Some poor pitiful person may say, "Think what I have gone through. Think what a terrible time we have had. Think how hard people have been on us." You may be tempted to follow him out of sympathy. No! Never follow someone unless his doctrine is right. This is a serious matter. Our Lord said, "Beware of those who are hypocrites. Beware of the leaven of hypocrisy."

Then we find what Christ said about the leaven of the Sadducees in Matthew 22:23, *"The same day came to him the Sadducees, which say that there is no resurrection."* The leaven of the Sadducees is false doctrine. They teach things that are not true. The Pharisees pretend to be people that they are not. The Sadducees openly deny the truth.

We do not have Pharisees and Sadducees as far as a distinct office of people today, but we have the same things going on. We have people who are not what they pretend to be and people teaching things that are false doctrine.

Let us understand also the third type of leaven. Mark 8:15 says, *"And he charged them, saying, Take heed, beware of the leaven of the Pharisees, and of the leaven of Herod."* The third leaven is the leaven of Herod. This speaks of the Herodian family, the family in power.

Herod the Great was appointed by the Ceasar to be king of the Jews in 37 B.C. The Herodian family dominated the political life of the "Holy Land" throughout the first century.

The leaven of Herod is worldliness. It is seeking after power. It is the idea of building religious coalitions which include unbelievers. It is the idea that God does His work the same way the world does its work. There is so much of this today among people in the ministry. People are employing the ways of the world to attempt the work of God.

> *Corrupting influences are always at work.*

We have been deceived into believing that we cannot do God's work without strength in numbers. When it comes to doctrine, when it comes to truth and the things of God, there must be no giving of ground whatsoever. We must have this vigilance concerning the truth.

If I said to you, "There is a restaurant in town where people are getting food poisoning; be careful about where you eat," every one of you would respond, "Please tell us the name of the restaurant!" But if I said, "There are people who are dangerous, and what they are teaching is dangerous; it is dangerous spiritually, and if you believe it, you could go to hell believing it, thinking that you are going to heaven!" So many people would say in response, "Please do not tell us. We do not want to cause division." Friends, we are not thinking biblically. We must adhere to the doctrine of Christ and compassionately warn against those who do not.

If a poisonous serpent coiled near a man, you may excite him by yelling, "Move!" But he would be glad for the warning. I do not want to be mean-spirited; I do not want to be crude with people; but we must be truthful.

Corrupting influences are always at work. We must pray that God will help us to discern these corrupting influences.

God's work is not done the same way the world's work is done. One of the great things we are going to have to deal with as a believing people is the issue of moralism. The outcry is that we need stronger morals, and we do. I am in the moral crowd. I want people to do what is morally right. But people do not go to heaven just because they do what is morally right. They must be born again of the Spirit of God.

We must love God's approval more than we love the approval of men.

I appreciate everyone who is living a clean, moral life. But the fixed point of reference for morality is the Word of God. We have people who are very hard on certain issues, but soft on others. Let us place the emphasis where God places the emphasis. The gospel is the power of God unto salvation.

Contention Sometimes Arises Even Among Brethren

This is painful, but it happens. Let us consider two prominent figures in Galatians chapter two–Peter and Paul. There was contention between them.

The Bible says in Galatians 2:8, *"For he that wrought effectually in Peter to the apostleship of the circumcision, the same was mighty in me toward the Gentiles."* That verse simply means that God gave Peter a ministry to the Jews, and God gave Paul a ministry to the Gentiles.

Verse nine says, *"And when James, Cephas, and John, who seemed to be pillars, perceived the grace that was given unto me, they gave to me and Barnabas the right hands of fellowship; that we should go unto the heathen, and they unto the circumcision."*

James, Cephas (or Peter), and John went to the circumcision, the Jews. Paul and Barnabas went to the Gentiles, preaching the gospel to them.

Then verse ten says, *"Only they would that we should remember the poor; the same which I also was forward to do."*

"Just take care of the poor," they added. "Yes, sir, we will be happy to do that!" I really do not think that Peter and the church in Jerusalem were in the place of exercising any authority over Paul. These were independent assemblies of people doing what God gave them to do. They simply recommended that they take care of the poor.

Verses eleven and twelve say,

> *But when Peter was come to Antioch, I withstood him to the face, because he was to be blamed. For before that certain came from James, he did eat with the Gentiles: but when they were come, he withdrew and separated himself, fearing them which were of the circumcision.*

Peter was with Paul in Antioch, and he was eating with the Gentiles. He heard that people were coming who might have a problem with him eating with the Gentiles, and so he changed his behavior and attitude about the matter.

Let me pause to mention that you and I are never going to accomplish what the apostle Peter accomplished. We are not down on Peter, but I want you to understand something. Why did God put such a thing in the Bible for us? Why would God tell us in His Word that two of the most prominent people in the first century had contention with each other? He is teaching us something! Let us read on.

Verse thirteen says, *"And the other Jews dissembled likewise with him; insomuch that Barnabas also was carried away with their dissimulation."*

Look what a problem this had become! Barnabas was working with Paul. Peter realized that there were people coming who were going to see him eating with the Gentiles, and he decided that he would withdraw from them, even though he said it was all right. It caused such a problem that other believers also withdrew. Barnabas even said, "I am following Peter!"

No doubt, there is much going on between verses thirteen and fourteen in the hearts and minds of these men. Contention was swirling in that assembly.

Verse fourteen says,

> *But when I saw that they walked not uprightly according to the truth of the gospel, I said unto Peter before them all, If thou, being a Jew, livest after the manner of Gentiles, and not as do the Jews, why compellest thou the Gentiles to live as do the Jews?*

Paul said, "I had to confront Peter to his face and say, 'This is not according to the truth!'" Now, these were both believers, and prominent believers. They were highly visible, men who were both blessed with marvelous ministries. Other people knew them. But there was contention between these brethren.

You may be saying, "I am going to get along with everyone." Wait a minute. Be careful. We all want to get along with everyone, but not by disregarding the truth. We must love God's approval more than we love the approval of men.

I have tried to follow after Christ. I have determined that the sole authority for our faith and practice is the Word of God. The only head of our church is Jesus Christ. Can you imagine through the years what this has cost me with some people? Friends, we must cast ourselves entirely on God's mercy. I want you to know that there is no painless way to follow Jesus Christ. His approval is all that matters.

If you are going to vigilantly guard doctrinal truth, there are going to be times of contention even among brethren. One of the big things that we are dealing with today is not the open denial of doctrine, but many of the common denominator church practices that are going on through musical programs and other types of things that are disregarding doctrine or placing doctrine secondary to experience or emotion. We must not let that take place in our churches.

People who are Spirit-filled are not boring, because it is God that is working in them and giving enthusiasm to them. Think of the Savior; think of the truth, before you get all emotionally worked-up about something and behave as if that is all you want.

Think about what you are going to be able to teach your children. Truth must be passed from generation to generation. It is not just about how good a time you are having in the church service. It is about what truth is being taught that you know lines up with Scripture, and you can receive that truth and teach it to the next generation.

Remember, our faith is a treasured heritage, not a contemporary experiment. This is essential! The first century church paid a great price to be true to God. We should be willing to pay a price to be obedient to God in this matter.

Contending for Doctrinal Truth Must Be Done in Every Generation

I remember saying to Dr. John R. Rice years ago, "Dr. Rice, it seems you have written about everything that needs to be written." Dr. Rice's answer was profound. He said, "I wrote it in my generation; someone else has to speak it and write it in each generation. Affirm again and again that this is where we stand!"

In Hebrews 5:11-14 the Bible says,

> *Of whom we have many things to say, and hard to be uttered, seeing ye are dull of hearing. For when for the time ye ought to be teachers, ye have need that one teach you again which be the first principles of the oracles of God; and are become such as have need of milk, and not of strong meat. For every one that useth milk is unskilful in the word of righteousness: for he is a babe. But strong meat belongeth to them that are of full age, even those who by reason of use have their senses exercised to discern both good and evil.*

Obviously some people do not think about their children or grandchildren the way they should when it comes to the things of God. To them, church is no more than a place to go to have fun.

What has happened to the sacred? Where is the reverence? What ever happened to sin? Most every "problem" has become an "addiction." What happened to *"lust"*? Who needs a Savior?

There is no painless way to follow Jesus Christ.

People say, "We are having fun!" And the idea is, "You boring people are not having any fun." The truth is, we have not made fun the goal; we have made God and God's truth the goal, but we have the joy of the Lord.

Remember the educational reading experiment where people never learned how to read. How sad! But think of that compared to how truly sad it is when people have experimented with the faith of our fathers–our godly heritage.

"Well, we went to church; we had a great time!" If you asked, "What did you learn about truth and the Bible?" they would reply, "We did not do much with doctrine because that divides." What are you going to give the next generation? What are you going to give your children and grandchildren?

These people have no discernment. How dangerous! If we are going to have a first century church, we must have first century doctrine. It must be contended for in every generation.

Jude 1-3 says,

> *Jude, the servant of Jesus Christ, and brother of James, to them that are sanctified by God the Father, and preserved in Jesus Christ, and called: mercy unto you, and peace, and love, be multiplied. Beloved, when I gave all diligence to write unto you of the common salvation, it was needful for me to write unto you, and exhort you that ye should earnestly contend for the faith which was once delivered unto the saints.*

Truth must be passed from generation to generation.

A friend of mine said, "I want you to be involved with us in a great political revival." I said to him, "I understand what you are trying to do, and I am going to try to get everyone I can to vote for what is morally right, but my energy and time is not going to be given to a political revival. I want to cast myself at the mercy of God and pray for a spiritual revival in my heart, my church, and my nation."

Jude said, "I am writing unto you about salvation," and many people interpret this to mean that he had a change of mind. On the contrary, he was saying, "If I am going to write unto you of the common salvation, if we are going to deal with the common salvation, then we must contend for the faith. If you do not contend for the faith, you are going to lose the message of salvation."

Notice again that Jude 3 says, *"Beloved, when I gave all diligence to write unto you of the common salvation, it was needful for me to write unto you, and exhort you that ye should earnestly contend for the faith which was once delivered unto the saints."* In other words, if you do not contend for the faith, there will not be any common salvation to talk about. We must contend for the faith in every generation.

Though our buildings are filled and properties are expanding and people are coming to Christ, never in your life discount the fact that faithful men are out in some unknown place preaching to eight or ten people week after week, declaring the truth of God's Word soundly. They cannot create some religious shopping center, and neither will we.

We believe that it is the responsibility of the preacher to declare the truth of God's Word line upon line, precept upon precept, and for families to take that truth into their homes and teach it to their children.

> *We do not need another imitation of the world.*

Some parent in a small church may say, "Well, I have to take my children somewhere they can really get something!" Get what? What is that something? If they are getting the truth there, stay and work to bring others. You can take your children to a ballgame. The church does not have to do that! You can take them on a picnic; the church does not have to do that! You had better thank God that they are getting the truth there! The church is the pillar and ground of the truth!

What have we done? Do we think that every church is supposed to mimic the world and do everything the world does? What have we done to our children? We do not need another imitation of the world.

Chapter Five

I read recently that only two out of every ten teenagers are even interested in going to church! Only four out of every ten children are in church anywhere faithfully in America. According to a recent survey by the Southern Baptist Convention, forty-seven churches close each week in America. Something is wrong–terribly wrong.

The church that has traded truth for pleasure has become a great harm to a hurting world.

The church that has traded truth for pleasure has become a great harm to a hurting world. If you do not believe the truth, you are going to miss heaven! Your kids may be super-charged and super-involved, but if they have never repented of their sin and trusted the Lord Jesus as their Savior, they are going to miss heaven! Nothing is worse than a generation of children with no faith in the true and living God.

The church is not about being some sort of nice, safe, social club! The New Testament church is about thundering forth the Word of God in the power of God's Holy Spirit and giving people a fixed point of reference to see that this is the truth of God. Stand with convictions bathed in compassion. Do not drift from this! You can build your life, your home, your family, your future, and your eternity on the truth of God's holy Word.

VI

The Structure of the First Century Church

here is a great deal of confusion concerning the church. Is one faith as good as another? As a Christian, I recognize the sole authority for our faith and practice is the Word of God. The Bible is our fixed point of reference. We judge all things by the truth of God's Word. Of course, this may appear to be very narrow minded to some people. But let us follow the Lord and be true to Him and His Word. Let us have His loving compassion toward others.

Let us be biblical. Let us stay with the Word of God. We will have our critics; we always have. But we should love them too and seek to tell them about the Savior.

The Bible says in Acts 2:41-47,

> *Then they that gladly received his word were baptized: and the same day there were added unto them about three thousand souls. And they continued stedfastly in the apostles' doctrine and fellowship,*

> *and in breaking of bread, and in prayers. And fear came upon every soul: and many wonders and signs were done by the apostles. And all that believed were together, and had all things common; and sold their possessions and goods, and parted them to all men, as every man had need. And they, continuing daily with one accord in the temple, and breaking bread from house to house, did eat their meat with gladness and singleness of heart, praising God, and having favour with all the people. And the Lord added to the church daily such as should be saved.*

In this passage we learn a great deal about the church. We must be true to the *message* of the first century church and to the *methods* of the first century church. *Means* certainly change, but our message and our methods must always be biblical.

The distinctive of the first century church was its obedience to the Word of God. We must examine all things by the Bible. We must ask, "Is this what the Bible teaches? Is this the clear teaching of God's Word?" Many times there is a family of Scriptures or a group of Scriptures that need to be placed together so that we may have the full idea of what God intends about a certain subject.

Remember Matthew 16:13-18,

> *When Jesus came into the coasts of Caesarea Philippi, he asked his disciples, saying, Whom do men say that I the Son of man am? And they said, Some say that thou art John the Baptist: some, Elias; and others, Jeremias, or one of the prophets. He saith unto them, But whom say ye that I am? And Simon Peter answered and said, Thou art the Christ, the Son of the living God. And Jesus answered and said unto him, Blessed art thou, Simon Barjona: for flesh and blood hath not revealed it unto thee, but my Father*

> *which is in heaven. And I say also unto thee, That thou art Peter, and upon this rock I will build my church; and the gates of hell shall not prevail against it.*

Christ said, *"I will build my church."*

The Bible says in Matthew 18:13-17,

> *And if so be that he find it, verily I say unto you, he rejoiceth more of that sheep, than of the ninety and nine which went not astray. Even so it is not the will of your Father which is in heaven, that one of these little ones should perish. Moreover if thy brother shall trespass against thee, go and tell him his fault between thee and him alone: if he shall hear thee, thou hast gained thy brother. But if he will not hear thee, then take with thee one or two more, that in the mouth of two or three witnesses every word may be established. And if he shall neglect to hear them, tell it unto the church: but if he neglect to hear the church, let him be unto thee as an heathen man and a publican.*

In these passages we certainly do not find everything that we need to know about church discipline and dealing with unruly people. A part of discipline is restoring people back into the fellowship of the local assembly following the guidelines in God's Word (Galatians 6:1). But the point I desire to make is that there was a structure in the first century church. There had to be some structure or there could have been no organized body to whom one could appeal. They were to tell it to the church.

It might be helpful to note that not one time in the Bible is the word *church* used for a national church. It is incorrect for us to speak collectively of "the church in America." It is not biblically correct to refer to a national church.

I want you to remember that the word *church* comes from the word *ekklesia* meaning, "called-out assembly." The Lord Jesus said, "I will build My called-out assembly."

The Mandate for the Structure of the First Century Church

The Lord Jesus commanded His disciples to go into all the world and preach the gospel to every creature. The gospel is the "good news." There is bad news, and the bad news is that the wages of sin is death. In light of that, the good news is that the gift of God is eternal life through Jesus Christ our Lord. Without the bad news concerning sin, the good news is no news at all.

We admire those who go out with the gospel, give clearly the message of salvation, and lead people as God leads them by His spirit to the saving knowledge of the Lord Jesus. But we are not to stop there. We are not only to seek the salvation of the lost; we are to make disciples and establish local churches. This is the mandate that God has given us.

The Bible says in Acts 2:41-42,

> *Then they that gladly received his word were baptized: and the same day there were added unto them about three thousand souls. And they continued stedfastly in the apostles' doctrine and fellowship, and in breaking of bread, and in prayers.*

When we consider this mandate, we must fulfill it the Bible way. We understand that this local assembly, this New Testament church, is made up only of redeemed people, people who have come to know the Lord Jesus Christ as their personal Savior.

You are going to find churches where that is not a requirement. But the Bible requires a regenerate membership for the local assembly. We are not talking about the congregation, we are not talking about everyone that comes together because there are more people coming together to hear the preaching of God's Word than there are making up that church, that local assembly.

People are welcome to come to the services; we want people to come and listen to God's Word. But according to the Scripture, the local church should be made up of people that have been born again by God's Spirit, who have been brought from death to life by the power of the Lord Jesus.

Without the bad news concerning sin, the good news is no news at all.

We understand that in this mandate we are also to obey Christ in baptism and continue in the apostles' doctrine, meaning that we are to follow the clear teaching of God's Word. We are to follow after the Word of God. The Bible says that they *"continued stedfastly in the apostles' doctrine."*

The Bible says in Colossians 1:17-18, *"And he is before all things, and by him all things consist. And he is the head of the body, the church: who is the beginning, the firstborn from the dead; that in all things he might have the preeminence."*

The only head of the local church is the Lord Jesus Christ. He is to have the preeminence in all things. This preeminence means He is not simply "one of" but the "one and only" in the church.

The Membership of the First Century Church

Some consider membership in a local church to be unimportant. Let us look at what the Bible says. We will look at the life of Paul for an example.

The Bible says in Acts 9:26, *"And when Saul was come to Jerusalem, he assayed to join himself to the disciples: but they were all afraid of him, and believed not that he was a disciple."*

Notice the word *"join."* The word means "to glue together or to cement together." Evidently, there was a local assembly that Paul recognized that was made up of disciples, and his desire was to *join* himself with them. But there was a problem; they were afraid of him.

The Bible says in Acts 9:27-29,

> *But Barnabas took him, and brought him to the apostles, and declared unto them how he had seen the Lord in the way, and that he had spoken to him, and how he had preached boldly at Damascus in the name of Jesus. And he was with them coming in and going out at Jerusalem. And he spake boldly in the name of the Lord Jesus, and disputed against the Grecians: but they went about to slay him.*

Barnabas stood up for him. Paul's desire was to join with them. Not simply to say, "I am going to casually come and go." He wanted to be solidly identified with that body. Paul went to that local assembly and said, "This is a church that is following God's mandate. This is a local assembly that is doing what the Bible says a church should do. This is a group of people who have solidly joined together and have decided under God that they are going to be obedient to Christ and give allegiance to Christ and Christ alone as the only head. I want to join them."

In Acts chapter four, the disciples were having difficulty. They were being persecuted for their faith. We read in Acts 4:23, *"And being let go, they went to their own company, and reported all that the chief priests and elders had said unto them."* Notice that there was some group to whom they could report. *"They went to their own company."*

The Bible says in Acts 5:12-14,

> *And by the hands of the apostles were many signs and wonders wrought among the people; (and they were all with one accord in Solomon's porch. And of the rest durst no man join himself to them: but the people magnified them. And believers were the more added to the Lord, multitudes both of men and women.)*

A strange thing happened in Acts chapter five. Ananias and Sapphira had been struck dead by the power of God and a great fear came upon that assembly. It was not so much a terrorizing fear or some sort of frightening thing as someone running from a fire or from a natural disaster. It was a fear in reverence and awe of God.

People gave very serious thought as to whether or not they wanted to join a group of people who were having such things happen. They understood from the outside looking in how serious a matter it was to be identified with God's people.

The preaching began. There was a large gathering on Solomon's porch, and in the congregation there was an assembly of people identified with this local New Testament church. Solomon's porch was a large space where they could gather to preach in the temple area. Being a part of this church was no longer just a popular thing that people were doing. They realized that there was something very serious about being identified with this local assembly of baptized believers.

Chapter Six

I say to you in all kindness that so little is being made of church membership in most places today that individual Christian people think they can hop from church to church and do as they please, never committing to anything. That is one of the main reasons why so little is actually being accomplished in the work of God today.

Let us consider another example concerning church membership. The Bible says in I Corinthians 5:9, *"I wrote unto you in an epistle not to company with fornicators."* This church in Corinth was having to deal with people in the church who were involved in sexual sin and immorality. Paul said in I Corinthians 5:9-10, *"I wrote unto you in an epistle not to company with fornicators: yet not altogether with the fornicators of this world, or with the covetous, or extortioners, or with idolaters; for then must ye needs go out of the world."*

This is such a powerful passage. Paul said, "I am not saying that you cannot have any contact with these people or the covetous, or the extortioners, or the idolaters." In other words, if you were going to get away from all sinners, you would have to leave the world. But, "You must deal with this in the church because of the testimony of the church." The testimony of Christ in that city was no more powerful than the testimony of that church.

No wonder people think so little of God! No wonder false religions are growing by leaps and bounds! The fastest growing religion in America is not Christianity; it is Islam. If churches were doing what they should do, if each local assembly was on fire with the Spirit of God, living the Christ-centered life, magnifying the Lord Jesus, taking seriously what God has given us to do, then there would be such a moving of God that little attention would be given to false religion. The Philistine temples were full when Samson was powerless.

Paul explained that it is one thing when sin is in the world; it is another thing when it is in the church. The Bible says in I Corinthians 5:11, *"But now I have written unto you not to keep company, if any man that is called a brother be a fornicator, or covetous, or an idolater, or a railer, or a drunkard, or an extortioner; with such an one no not to eat."*

If there comes a time when there is a disorderly brother who is divisive or engaged in one of these named sins or something else we know to be in direct disobedience to God, the Bible says that we must not even eat with him. It sounds cruel, but that is how much God is concerned about His name and the testimony of His people in this world.

The Bible says in I Corinthians 5:12, *"For what have I to do to judge them also that are without? do not ye judge them that are within?"* I would like for you to notice the word *"without"* and the word *"within."* The next verse says, *"But them that are without God judgeth. Therefore put away from among yourselves that wicked person."*

Paul declared that if there is someone in the world, lost without God and without hope, God will deal with that person. But in the local assembly of baptized believers that people mutually agree to be a part of, it is important that the testimony of that church be upheld and that sin be dealt with inside that church.

I say to you in all kindness that so little is being made of church membership in most places today that individual Christian people think they can hop from church to church and do as they please, never committing to anything. That is one of the main reasons why so little is actually being accomplished in the work of God today.

No local church should ever join anything. We should not be joining denominational groups; a church should not be joining fellowships. Pastors may fellowship with other pastors as long as the fellowship is a *verb* and not a *noun*. But we should never institutionalize that fellowship, because once we align ourselves with it, the one thing someone does in it that is disobedient to God drags everyone else into that disobedience. In the local church this issue can be dealt with as we follow God's disciplinary direction.

The testimony of Christ in that city was no more powerful than the testimony of that church.

We are free people. We are to remain free from all unholy alliances. Our allegiance is to Christ and Christ alone.

It is important to understand that there was a group without and a group within. If there was a group without and a group within, evidently they had membership and they mutually agreed to certain things that they would follow and a body of truth they would adhere to.

The Metaphors Used to Describe the First Century Church

I am emphasizing several metaphors because these figures of speech are used in the Bible. There are one-word expressions that give clarity to what we are all about. Let me give you a few that help explain the structure of the New Testament church.

The Body of Christ

This first metaphor is the *body*. This local assembly is a body. We only have one head, and that head is the Lord Jesus.

The Bible says in I Corinthians 12:12, *"For as the body is one, and hath many members, and all the members of that one body, being many, are one body: so also is Christ."*

The Bible says in I Corinthians 12:26, *"And whether one member suffer, all the members suffer with it; or one member be honoured, all the members rejoice with it."*

Think how precious this metaphor reveals the local church to be. As members grieve over the loss of loved ones who have died, we grieve with them; we sorrow with them. We also rejoice with them that their loved ones are with the Lord. They are a part of our body.

When we enter into this body, we are all members of this one body. You could not imagine that I would attack a member of my own body. Should I take an axe in one hand and chop off the other hand? Should I do something terribly detrimental with one part of my body to another part of my body?

When I am living in obedience to what I know to be true in my head, I would never do such a thing. When we are in obedience to our Head, the Lord Jesus Christ, we will treat every member of this body the way every member of the body should be treated.

Again, the Bible says in I Corinthians 12:26, *"And whether one member suffer, all the members suffer with it; or one member be honoured, all the members rejoice with it."*

From time to time our members suffer. All of the members suffer. How many of you have ever known a member to be honored? When that member is honored, all of the members rejoice over that honor. They are not jealous over the honor that member receives; they rejoice over that honor.

We understand when we truly have a church like God wants it to be, then we suffer together, we rejoice together, we praise God together. It is a wonderful thing to be one body. That is what the Lord has given us in the local church.

Chapter Six

The Household of God

One of these expressions God gives to our local assembly is *"household."* The Bible says in Ephesians 2:19, *"Now therefore ye are no more strangers and foreigners, but fellowcitizens with the saints, and of the household of God."*

We are a family, a *household*. This is a metaphor. I have a household, and I am the head of our household. My wife and I had the privilege of rearing two children for the Lord in our household. I was not more important than my wife, and we were not more important than our children as far as value is concerned. As far as structure and function is concerned, someone had to be the head in that household. Here is something beautiful that God teaches us in this household of faith–the household of God. The pastor is not, as far as value to God, more valuable than any other member. The Lord loves us all.

Think of the Old Testament priest who wore the name of every tribe engraved on beautiful stones on a breastplate. There were also six tribes on one shoulder and six tribes on the other shoulder. He loved each of them individually, as displayed on his breastplate. But he loved all of them equally, as demonstrated by them being distributed equally on each shoulder. God loves all of us individually, but He also loves us all equally.

In order to function as a household, someone must lead. That is why we find a whole body of Scriptures in the New Testament about a pastor leading, a pastor ruling, a pastor being the bishop and overseer. The people in willing submission understand that we need a pastor and the pastor leads in this local household. We treat one another as a family because we are a family.

I am grateful that we can forgive in a family. We do not hold grudges in a family. We do not bring up the sins of the past in a family. Think how beautiful, how spiritually beautiful a church truly is when it behaves as a *household*. I am glad to be part of a household like that.

We pray for one another in our household. We are tender with one another. When we are ill, we care for one another. When we are weak, we help carry the load for one another. If someone in your household is incapable at present of doing something that is a normal part of his routine, you help with that routine. You get under that load. That is a household; that is a family. It is a wonderful thing that God has structured the church this way. This was modeled for us in the first century church.

We are not to have churches within the church, just as we are not to have a household within a household. I mean by this that we are one household. All are members of the same household. Never take actions that will divide the household and create schisms in the household.

The Building of God

The Bible says in Ephesians 2:20-21, *"And are built upon the foundation of the apostles and prophets, Jesus Christ himself being the chief corner stone; in whom all the building fitly framed together groweth unto an holy temple in the Lord."*

Another metaphor used in reference to the church is a *building*. The Lord Jesus is the foundation. Do you know that in a building, the parts for the building are of little value when separated? You could take stones for a foundation and put them on the ground, but they must be put in the foundation of the building to be of most value. You may take the windows out and lay them somewhere on the ground, and the windows are of some value; but they are of very little value until they are placed where they should be placed in the building. God says that we are a building and we are fitly joined together.

The Bible says in Ephesians 4:14-16,

> *That we henceforth be no more children, tossed to and fro, and carried about with every wind of doctrine, by the sleight of men, and cunning craftiness, whereby they lie in wait to deceive; but speaking the truth in*

love, may grow up into him in all things, which is the head, even Christ: from whom the whole body fitly joined together and compacted by that which every joint supplieth, according to the effectual working in the measure of every part, maketh increase of the body unto the edifying of itself in love.

These are just some of the metaphors–a body, a household, a building. The Lord uses these beautiful words to tell us more and more of what He expects each local church to be. As we follow God's Word, the church can be a colony of heaven on earth for just awhile until we meet our Savior face to face.

I love the local church. I love being a member, and I am willing to adhere to the body of doctrine we have found in the Bible. I love behaving like a member should behave, because it is not only beneficial to me; it is also beneficial to all others–to the body.

When someone needs to be disciplined, then God has told us how to discipline a person in the membership. If you ever leave your local church and you are going to identify with another local assembly, you should make sure it is an independent assembly. Make sure it is free from all allegiances that would corrupt and all things that hinder and harm and enter in to bring reproach to the Lord. You should make sure it is an assembly that adheres to the Bible as the sole authority for faith and practice. You should make sure that they believe that the membership should adhere to Scripture, and that when the members do not adhere to Scripture, they should deal with that matter.

It is a beautiful thing to represent our Lord Jesus Christ in the local church, which is His body. When we assemble together, we hear the Word of God, and that helps us to know what we should be. As we leave the place of assembly, we should go out and behave ourselves as Jesus Christ would have us behave. The local church moves forward doing God's work God's way, seeking to win the lost.

I want to become a first century Christian in every way and be a part of a first century church. I want to know what the Bible says about it so I can say, "Lord, I want to live in obedience to Your Word." I thank God that we have this mandate, that we understand this membership, and that we have these beautiful metaphors to teach us.

VII

The Prayer Life of the First Century Church

he Lord Jesus taught His disciples to pray. He taught them how to get their prayers answered. In Acts chapter one, we come to a scene on the Mount of Olives describing the Lord Jesus Christ's ascension. As He is taken out of sight, angels stand by and say, *"Ye men of Galilee, why stand ye gazing up into heaven? this same Jesus, which is taken up from you into heaven, shall so come in like manner as ye have seen him go into heaven"* (Acts 1:11).

We are to look for and love the appearing of Jesus Christ. I hope that you have the right attitude about the Second Coming of Christ. The quality of your Christian life is determined by your outlook–looking to Him and looking for Him. Our hope is not in the Second Coming of Christ but in the Christ of the Second Coming.

Can you imagine walking with the Lord Jesus here on earth, or being one of those in His family? His mother, for example, knew what no other human being knew: no man had anything to do with the birth of this One. She stood at Calvary and watched Jesus Christ bleed and die. He was her own Son, the One she gave birth to. She was the vessel God had chosen to bring forth what He sent forth into the world.

> *Our hope is not in the Second Coming of Christ but in the Christ of the Second Coming.*

Mary did not cry out in some psychological rage, "Come down from there! Let me tell you the truth!" No, she stood there in silence with absolute confidence in God knowing that He was the virgin-born Son of God. She had to put her faith in Christ just as all others have to put their faith in Christ for their soul's salvation.

Think of being with Him, loving Him, following Him. And now He had ascended to heaven out of their sight.

The Bible says in Acts 1:12-14,

> *Then returned they unto Jerusalem from the mount called Olivet, which is from Jerusalem a sabbath day's journey. And when they were come in, they went up into an upper room, where abode both Peter, and James, and John, and Andrew, Philip, and Thomas, Bartholomew, and Matthew, James the son of Alphaeus, and Simon Zelotes, and Judas the brother of James. These all continued with one accord in prayer and supplication, with the women, and Mary the mother of Jesus, and with his brethren.*

The first century church continued in prayer. As we search the Scriptures, we find the church meeting in two distinctively different kinds of meetings. They gathered together for the teaching and preaching of the Word of God. This is evident as we read the epistles of Paul and the book of Acts.

The second kind of meeting we find in the New Testament is one that churches today have sadly neglected. We must admit to our own shame in this area. The most necessary meeting you find the church having in the New Testament was a prayer meeting. This necessary meeting is the most neglected.

In Ephesians 5:20 the Bible says, *"Giving thanks always for all things unto God and the Father in the name of our Lord Jesus Christ."* We are to pray to the Father in the name of the Lord Jesus Christ.

Praying to the Father is something I think we understand. We can call God our Father. The Bible says in Romans 8:14-15, *"For as many as are led by the Spirit of God, they are the sons of God. For ye have not received the spirit of bondage again to fear; but ye have received the Spirit of adoption, whereby we cry, Abba, Father."*

We are not children of God by nature; we are children of the Devil by nature. Every human being is stillborn spiritually. No one is a child of God by nature. We must receive a new nature. It is not something we inherit. We must be born into God's family. God becomes our Father as we become His children by faith, repenting of our sin and trusting Christ as Savior.

The Bible says we are to pray to the Father in the name of the Lord Jesus Christ. Often we say when we pray, "In Jesus' name." We should not use only the human title. We should pray as we are instructed, *"in the name of our Lord Jesus Christ,"* combining all three of these titles. Why? Because we are speaking of the victorious One, our conquering Christ, our ascended Lord.

The Bible says in Hebrews chapter twelve that we are to look unto Jesus *"the author and finisher of our faith."* When you look unto the Lord, what Christ are you looking to? When you imagine that you are looking to the Lord Jesus, what do you imagine? The Bible teaches us in Hebrews 8:1, *"Now of the things which we have spoken this is the sum: We have such an high priest, who is set on the right hand of the throne of the Majesty in the heavens."*

The Bible uses the word *"sum."* This is the total. This is all. The Christ we look to is the victorious, seated Savior, coequal, coexistent, eternally existent with God the Father and God the Holy Spirit. I believe this is the One we are to look to. When we pray in the name of our Lord Jesus Christ, we are declaring the authority that He has. He has satisfied every demand of a Holy God. He has satisfied every demand made by the Law. He has purchased our salvation with His own blood. Salvation is full, free, and forever. He lives forevermore seated in heaven. He is our risen Savior. He is God. He is Christ. Christ is God, coequal, coexistent with God the Father and God the Holy Spirit. We look to Him.

When we pray in the name of our Lord Jesus Christ, there is no higher name, no greater name by which we may pray. No other name has more authority than His name.

When we pray in the name of our Lord Jesus Christ, there is no higher name, no greater name by which we may pray. No other name has more authority than His name. He is our conquering Christ. The praying church understands this.

We face many enemies and obstacles. The songwriter had it right, "Through many dangers, toils, and snares..." We need authority and there is no higher authority than our Lord Jesus Christ. This is the way we should pray.

We need a praying church. We should pray together as a church. Of course, I believe in individual prayers. But we should meet together for prayer. There must be meetings that are planned and an agenda from which we approach the Lord. Collectively, we believe as a church that these are things for which we need to pray and seek God's face. The praying church must collectively come together to pray and go to the Father in the name of our Lord Jesus Christ for specific things.

A praying church is like a body that is functioning properly. People are not going in different directions. A praying church is functioning as a group of baptized believers who have voluntarily joined themselves together to do the work that God has given that local congregation to do. He gives a pastor to lead the church. The pastor is to be led by the Spirit of God.

Many churches will not allow a pastor to lead. As a matter of fact, there are many strong people, men and women, in churches who cannot lead and will not follow.

Of course, we believe in the priesthood of every believer. We have "individual soul liberty." This is a gift from God. But there is something very pleasing to God when a church prays together and works together, going to the Father in the name of our Lord Jesus Christ.

We will never accomplish what must be accomplished for the Lord and His glory, it will never be accomplished without being a praying church.

The early disciples realized how important this was. There were many arguments going on in the church. Of course, there rose a murmuring among the widows. It was a problem that had to be addressed. Consider the testimony of the disciples in Acts 6:4, *"But we will give ourselves continually to prayer, and to the ministry of the word."*

We actually declare by our lack of praying that we do not need God.

If we were making that statement, we may say, "We want to give ourselves to the ministry of the Word and prayer." But there is a divine order here. We cannot minister the Word of God without first praying. We cannot know God's Book without knowing the God who wrote it and conversing with Him and knowing Him and walking with Him.

If we said that there are certain things sadly lacking in our lives, most of us would have to put praying at the top of the list. In this day and age we think we have learned everything we need to learn and we know how to get everything done. We force our way through life instead of faithing our way through life. We actually declare by our lack of praying that we do not need God.

Life's greatest failures are those things we call successes that are not in the will of God.

The truth is, God will allow us to attempt to live without Him and will let us see what we can accomplish. There are many things being done without God that bring no glory to God and much glory to men. These are fruits that do not last. They soon rot. They are not of the Lord. Life's greatest failures are those things we call successes that are not in the will of God.

The first century church was a praying church. I want to have a praying church. As a pastor, I must take the time to teach the Word of God and lead others by example in this matter of prayer.

The First Century Church Declared Its Absolute Dependence Upon God

There should be regular times when the church is called together to do nothing but pray. The first century church declared its absolute dependence upon God.

The Bible says in Acts 1:14, *"These all continued with one accord in prayer and supplication, with the women, and Mary the mother of Jesus, and with his brethren."*

If we were having a preaching meeting, a meeting to teach the Word of God, I would say that in that meeting, only the men should do the preaching and teaching to a mixed audience. I believe I could show you from the Bible that men are to do that. But in this prayer meeting, I think you would be hard pressed to prove that these women were not praying.

Let me take it a step further. I believe they were praying audibly. As a matter of fact, if they were part of the church, and they were, they came together as a church to pray.

If the Lord had not spoken to them the way He had spoken to them and told them they were not orphans, they would have felt as if they were orphans. Christ was gone. They were all alone. This was something new. Though God has always had a people, the church did not exist in the Old Testament. It started with Christ and His disciples. The church age had a beginning and the church age will have an ending. God has always had a people, but the church was a sacred secret and was revealed as Christ was rejected as the king of the Jews.

This church prayed. They needed to know what to do. They came together and prayed as a church. That is what a praying church does; it does not run ahead, but waits on the Lord. We never waste time waiting on God. He is never late. Sometimes we are early, but He is never late.

We never waste time waiting on God. He is never late.

Chapter Seven

The First Century Church Sought God for Laborers Through Prayer

In Matthew 9:37-38 the first century church sought God for laborers. The Bible says, *"Then saith he unto his disciples, The harvest truly is plenteous, but the labourers are few; pray ye therefore the Lord of the harvest, that he will send forth labourers into his harvest."*

Where is the Lord's harvest? Is the harvest only in your area? No, the harvest field is the world.

When the praying church seeks God for laborers, God will hear and send laborers. We do not have laborers because we do not ask for them.

When we hear about a great need, we should pray as a church. We should bring it to the attention of the whole church, not one or two people, and pray for laborers. This is what a praying church does.

The First Century Church Came Together as One Body in Agreement Through Prayer

Notice again in the Gospel according to Matthew chapter eighteen that the Lord gives specific instruction about church discipline.

Consider what the Bible says in verses nineteen and twenty,

> *Again I say unto you, That if two of you shall agree on earth as touching any thing that they shall ask, it shall be done for them of my Father which is in*

heaven. For where two or three are gathered together in my name, there am I in the midst of them.

This promise is made to the smallest, plural company one could possibly have. The application here is the church praying together, binding things together. The first century church came together as one body in agreement.

Churches do not agree because they do not pray together. Praying together as a church will have the same effect that praying together as a family will have.

There was something going on that was very troubling in Matthew chapter eighteen. Someone had to be disciplined, and the church was about to be divided. There would be the possibility of some real conflict. The Devil would like to tear things apart and make the divide even greater. But this praying church came together in agreement as they prayed and sought God's face. The first century church was a praying church.

It is right to voice this agreement as we hear the prayers of others. We acknowledge our agreement by saying "Amen" in our hearts and with our lips to the prayers of those who express the desire of our hearts. We have power in prayer as we agree and bind things together in prayer to God.

The First Century Church Sought God's Protection Through Prayer

In Matthew 26:41 our Lord Jesus said, *"Watch and pray, that ye enter not into temptation: the spirit indeed is willing, but the flesh is weak."* The first century church sought protection from God.

The Lord Jesus said to His disciples, *"Watch and pray, that ye enter not into temptation."*

When I hear of someone I love dearly who has sinned, I immediately think, "Did I pray for him?" and I think, "Did we pray for him as we should have prayed for him?"

Do you pray for your pastor like you should pray for your pastor? Do you pray for others who serve God in the church? Do you know who they are? Do you pray for them?

What shock and hurt churches go through when a moral failure enters the life of someone who is in leadership. We must pray for people.

The praying church seeks God for His guiding and protecting hand. We must pray for the children of our church. We must pray for the youth that God will protect them, not just the ones in our household, but all the young people of the church family.

Pray specifically for these that affect the testimony of your church. Pray for people on the job that they will keep their minds clean and have a strong witness for Christ.

A praying church realizes that the Devil is out there and he is trying to do everything he can to bring his greatest temptation across our path at our weakest moment. The only way to win the victory is through prayer.

The First Century Church Had Increased Faith and Enlarged Vision Through Prayer

The first century church sought God and had increased faith and enlarged vision. In Acts 4, we find that the disciples were told by religious leaders who opposed them not to do what they were doing any longer. A great miracle had taken place and persecution was brought on because of it. In Acts 4:23-24 the Bible says,

> *And being let go, they went to their own company, and reported all that the chief priests and elders had said unto them. And when they heard that, they lifted up their voice to God with one accord, and said, Lord, thou art God, which hast made heaven, and earth, and the sea, and all that in them is.*

They began to quote Scripture in their prayer, which is a wonderful thing. They quoted the Psalms in their prayer. They continued to pray in verses twenty-five through twenty-nine,

> *Who by the mouth of thy servant David hast said, Why did the heathen rage, and the people imagine vain things? The kings of the earth stood up, and the rulers were gathered together against the Lord, and against his Christ. For of a truth against thy holy child Jesus, whom thou hast anointed, both Herod, and Pontius Pilate, with the Gentiles, and the people of Israel, were gathered together, for to do whatsoever thy hand and thy counsel determined before to be done. And now, Lord, behold their threatenings: and grant unto thy servants, that with all boldness they may speak thy word.*

This is the behavior of a praying church. Do you recognize what they did? They did not look at themselves. They did not look at flesh matched against flesh. They looked to heaven and said, *"Thou art God!"* and their faith was increased and their vision enlarged.

I go to churches that have little or no faith and have no vision. Do you know why? They do not pray because they do not look to the Lord. When we turn our eyes upon the Lord, our faith increases and our vision enlarges. Find a man that has been with God and he will have the heart of God for things.

Do you want that kind of church? You can be a part of that kind of church if you will pay the price in prayer.

The First Century Church Faced Great Trials Through Prayer

In Acts chapter twelve, a mighty leader in the church, James the brother of John, was killed. They thought it was such a good idea to kill James, they decided to kill Peter also.

The Bible says in Acts 12:5, *"Peter therefore was kept in prison: but prayer was made without ceasing of the church unto God for him."*

If you have read the story, you know that Peter was miraculously delivered. The first century church faced times of great trial through prayer. When they prayed, Peter was miraculously delivered.

Acts 12:12 says, *"And when he had considered the thing, he came to the house of Mary the mother of John, whose surname was Mark; where many were gathered together praying."*

Charles Haddon Spurgeon said that, when Peter got out of jail and he was miraculously delivered, he knew exactly where to go because he knew they were having a prayer meeting in Mary's house. Peter made a beeline for Mary's house in Jerusalem. He waited at the door.

Rhoda came to the door, and after seeing Peter, ran to tell the others that he was standing at the door.

THE FIRST CENTURY CHURCH SOUGHT GOD FOR OPPORTUNITIES TO GET OUT THE GOSPEL THROUGH PRAYER

In Colossians 4:1-3 the Bible says,

> *Masters, give unto your servants that which is just and equal; knowing that ye also have a Master in heaven. Continue in prayer, and watch in the same with thanksgiving; withal praying also for us, that God would open unto us a door of utterance, to speak the mystery of Christ, for which I am also in bonds.*

The followers of our Lord Jesus were taught by Him that they could receive what they needed from God through prayer. This was the Bible method they employed in times of need.

The first century church sought God for opportunities to get out the gospel. Would it be stretching it to say that our message must always be biblical and our methods must always be biblical? So much has gone on unguarded because people have been convinced that methods do not have to be biblical. Yes, methods must be as biblical as the message.

The means can change, but the message and the methods must always be biblical. For example, if I lived one hundred years ago, I would use a horse and buggy to get somewhere. Now I can get on a plane and fly there. I can speak on one side of America in the morning and the other side of the nation in the evening. But I am doing the same thing. I am traveling. I am preaching the same message and using the same methods but just using a different means of getting there.

We should seek God in our churches to lead us and show us how to get out the gospel never violating our biblical message or our biblical methods. For example, God led our church to live-stream our meetings by means of the internet. People from more than 170 countries have watched at one time or another.

Prayer is declaring our absolute dependence upon God.

We prayed earnestly about how to reach the university campuses. We sought God and said, "There's a city within a city, with 26,000 students on one campus." People told us we could not get in. We are not only there witnessing every week, we are also having services each week on that campus. Many are attending our church meetings and coming to know Christ as Savior. This happens through prayer.

The "powers that be" said it was impossible to have Bible clubs in public schools. We are in now in thirty-one of the public schools in our city. God opened the door through prayer. By the way, we must keep these doors open through prayer. Prayer is declaring our absolute dependence upon God.

I am sure there are many other things we could do to spread the gospel. How will churches get the message out? How will we know how to get this message out? The Bible teaches in Colossians 4:2-3 that we pray for God to give us direction. That is what a praying church does.

Do you want to be a part of a praying church? Believe God for great things! Hudson Taylor, founder of the China Inland Mission and a man mightily used of God, chose as his motto, "God is always advancing." Let us advance in prayer.

VIII

True Worship in the First Century Church

od and God alone is worthy of our worship. The Bible tells us that the Lord Jesus Christ traveled through the land of Samaria and met a woman at the well. In this meeting there is so much revealed to us concerning salvation and the worship of our God. We read the story in John 4:1-26,

> *When therefore the Lord knew how the Pharisees had heard that Jesus made and baptized more disciples than John, (though Jesus himself baptized not, but his disciples,) he left Judæa, and departed again into Galilee. And he must needs go through Samaria. Then cometh he to a city of Samaria, which is called Sychar, near to the parcel of ground that Jacob gave to his son Joseph. Now Jacob's well was there. Jesus therefore, being wearied with his journey, sat thus on the well: and it was about the sixth hour. There cometh a woman of Samaria to draw water: Jesus saith unto*

her, Give me to drink. (For his disciples were gone away unto the city to buy meat.) Then saith the woman of Samaria unto him, How is it that thou, being a Jew, askest drink of me, which am a woman of Samaria? for the Jews have no dealings with the Samaritans. Jesus answered and said unto her, If thou knewest the gift of God, and who it is that saith to thee, Give me to drink; thou wouldest have asked of him, and he would have given thee living water. The woman saith unto him, Sir, thou hast nothing to draw with, and the well is deep: from whence then hast thou that living water? Art thou greater than our father Jacob, which gave us the well, and drank thereof himself, and his children, and his cattle? Jesus answered and said unto her, Whosoever drinketh of this water shall thirst again: but whosoever drinketh of the water that I shall give him shall never thirst; but the water that I shall give him shall be in him a well of water springing up into everlasting life. The woman saith unto him, Sir, give me this water, that I thirst not, neither come hither to draw. Jesus saith unto her, Go, call thy husband, and come hither. The woman answered and said, I have no husband. Jesus said unto her, Thou hast well said, I have no husband: for thou hast had five husbands; and he whom thou now hast is not thy husband: in that saidst thou truly. The woman saith unto him, Sir, I perceive that thou art a prophet. Our fathers worshipped in this mountain; and ye say, that in Jerusalem is the place where men ought to worship. Jesus saith unto her, Woman believe me, the hour cometh, when ye shall neither in this mountain, nor yet at Jerusalem, worship the Father. Ye worship ye know not what: we know what we worship: for salvation is of the Jews. But the hour

> *cometh, and now is, when the true worshippers shall worship the Father in spirit and in truth: for the Father seeketh such to worship him. God is a Spirit: and they that worship him must worship him in spirit and in truth. The woman saith unto him, I know that Messias cometh, which is called Christ: when he is come, he will tell us all things. Jesus saith unto her, I that speak unto thee am he.*

In this particular account, many fascinating things call for our attention. Our Lord said when speaking to this woman in verse twenty-three, *"The hour cometh, and now is, when the true worshippers shall worship the Father in spirit and in truth: for the Father seeketh such to worship him."* Take note of the expression, *"true worshippers."* I sincerely desire to be a true worshipper of the living God. It is my desire that you be a true worshipper of the Lord Jesus Christ.

Are you a true worshipper of the Lord Jesus Christ? So much is taking place in many churches in the name of worship that is not true worship. If people go to the church house and they have a Bible and some of the words of their songs seem to be religious words, does that mean they are having worship?

Let me be the first to agree with you if you would like to make the point that the meetings of our church, when we come together collectively and corporately in order to worship the Lord, are not the only places that we worship. We do worship God alone in our hearts, adoring Him, praising Him, and entering into His presence. However, we find in the New Testament the local church coming together and worshipping the Lord as they prayed to Him and preached His Word. Speaking of the church in Jerusalem, the Bible says in Acts 2:42-47,

> *And they continued stedfastly in the apostles' doctrine and fellowship, and in breaking of bread, and in prayers. And fear came upon every soul: and*

many wonders and signs were done by the apostles. And all that believed were together, and had all things common; and sold their possessions and goods, and parted them to all men, as every man had need. And they, continuing daily with one accord in the temple, and breaking bread from house to house, did eat their meat with gladness and singleness of heart, praising God, and having favour with all the people. And the Lord added to the church daily such as should be saved.

The Bible says in verse forty-seven that as this assembly met together they praised God. They adored the Lord. They entered into His presence and worshipped Him.

> *Despite the Samaritan woman's wicked past, she had a divine appointment. She did not know it, but she had an appointment to meet the Son of God at this well.*

We set aside a place to meet, and we normally call it a church building. We come together on the Lord's Day to have what we refer to as worship. We indicate by our conversation that we are there to worship the Lord. I think all of us know that the activities that take place in many buildings called "church buildings" are far from true worship.

God has made us so that we might be able to worship Him once we have been redeemed by His precious blood. As a matter of fact, our God has designed us to be worshippers of the true and living God. It is impossible for us to be the followers of the Lord that we should be unless we are worshippers of the true and living God.

Our service to the Lord should grow out of our worship of Him. As a matter of fact, our service to the Lord, the work we do for Him, develops with the right motive as we worship our God.

God the Son Seeks

We have a God who seeks after us. The Bible says of the Lord Jesus, *"He must needs go through Samaria."* As He came to the well, this woman came at noonday to draw water. She came at noonday because she did not want to be seen. She was a woman who was living in adultery. She previously had five husbands, and she was living with a man who was not her husband. She was the outcast of the city. She did not want to be around other people because they knew what kind of woman she was.

Despite the Samaritan woman's wicked past, she had a divine appointment. She did not know it, but she had an appointment to meet the Son of God at this well because Jesus Christ was going to win her to Himself. He sought her.

Notice a part of their conversation. The Bible says in verses seven through ten,

> *There cometh a woman of Samaria to draw water: Jesus saith unto her, Give me to drink. (For his disciples were gone away unto the city to buy meat.) Then saith the woman of Samaria to him, How is it that thou, being a Jew, askest drink of me, which am a woman of Samaria? for the Jews have no dealings with the Samaritans. Jesus answered and said unto her, If thou knewest the gift of God, and who it is that saith to thee, Give me to drink; thou wouldest have asked of him, and he would have given thee living water.*

First, the Lord Jesus said, *"If thou knewest the gift of God..."* The unsaved do not know the gift of God. This verse speaks of salvation through God's Son. It is the work of those who know the Lord to make the gift of salvation known to those who do not know the Lord.

It is the work of those who know the Lord to make the gift of salvation known to those who do not know the Lord.

We are to speak of God's unspeakable gift and tell a lost world, *"For God so loved the world, that he gave his only begotten Son, that whosoever believeth in him should not perish, but have everlasting life"* (John 3:16).

We have been distracted from the great work God has given us to do–to make this gift known. *"For God so loved...that he gave."* The Lord Jesus paid the price for our sins with His own precious blood on the cross.

Second, the Lord Jesus said, "You do not know *'who it is that saith to thee, Give me to drink.'* You do not know the Lord Jesus Christ." Our Lord worked in this conversation to help this woman know the gift of God and know who He is.

As we are witnessing to people, it is our work to dwell on these two things–to help people know what the gift of God is and who Jesus Christ is. He is the eternal God–coequal, coexistent with God the Father and God the Holy Spirit. He offers the gift of salvation to all who will receive Him.

As the conversation continued, Jesus Christ made the Samaritan woman aware of her need. The great evidence that God is working in someone's life is the work of the Holy Spirit convicting of sin. Christ asked her about her husband. He brought the subject of sin into view.

People cannot be saved until they know they need a Savior. People must be aware of their sin and that their sin separates them from

God. Every human being is lost in sin, separated from God because of that sin. The wages of sin is death and hell, and the only payment God will accept is the payment of His own dear Son who bled and died for our sins upon the cross. When Christ died, He said, *"It is finished."* He paid our sin debt in full. This is the only payment God will accept–not our good works. The Bible says that your works and my works, though they may be good works in our eyes, are all nothing more than filthy rags in the sight of God (Isaiah 64:6).

The Lord Jesus sought this Samaritan woman. He was seeking for her to know the gift of God. He was seeking for her to know who He is.

God the Father Seeks

In John 4:19 we find that this woman wanted to change the subject. She said, *"Sir, I perceive that thou art a prophet."* She began to talk about worship. The conversation continued in verses twenty through twenty-three,

> *Our fathers worshipped in this mountain; and ye say, that in Jerusalem is the place where men ought to worship. Jesus saith unto her, Woman, believe me, the hour cometh, when ye shall neither in this mountain, nor yet at Jerusalem, worship the Father. Ye worship ye know not what: we know what we worship: for salvation is of the Jews. But the hour cometh, and now is, when the true worshippers shall worship the Father in spirit and in truth: for the Father seeketh such to worship him.*

Perhaps we have read this passage so many times in our devotional reading and missed the last expression in the verse. We know from passages like Luke 19:10 that *"the Son of man is come to seek and to save that which was lost."* We often talk about Jesus Christ seeking after sinners as He was seeking after this sinner. He is seeking sinners so that they might know the gift of God and know who He is–that He is the Christ and the only Savior. He is seeking sinners.

God the Father is also seeking those who have been redeemed and born into God's family to worship Him. This is clearly what the Bible says, *"The Father seeketh such to worship him."*

Did you know that only men who are redeemed can worship the Lord? The unsaved cannot worship the Lord. What are the implications of this? Only the redeemed can worship the Lord because it is the activity of the spirit of the redeemed. It is the action of a redeemed group of people to worship the Lord. The Father seeks people to worship Him. They must be redeemed people, or they cannot worship the Lord.

Remember, everything we do *for* God should come out of our worship *of* God. In other words, we should do what we do because of what God has done for us and because of what we know of the Lord. We love, adore, and worship the Lord. All that we do for the Lord should come out of our worship of God.

You cannot be a true worshipper of the Father unless you have been saved. However, many churches conduct services that are designed to attract the unsaved. Worldly music is brought in and worldly things are done. The whole program of the service is so much like the world that it is what the world is accustomed to hearing and seeing. The people who plan these services get the idea that this is what the unsaved want and this is what they will respond to. So, they make the church worldly to attract the world and bring the world into the church. They call this a church service. A church service is not necessarily a worship service. You cannot worship God unless you have been redeemed. Remember, the church house is only a place for the church to meet. It is not the church. Each individual must meet the Lord.

Yes, we should be seeking the lost and going after the unsaved. We are to go out into the highways and hedges, but I do not believe that we are to make our services worldly in order to bring in all the world. The world cannot worship God. Only those who have been redeemed can worship God.

A.W. Tozer stated more than fifty years ago,

> Pastors and churches in our hectic times are harassed by the temptation to seek size at any cost and to secure by inflation what they cannot gain by legitimate growth. They are greedy for thrills, and since they dare no longer seek them in the theater, they demand to have them brought into the church. A church fed on excitement is no New Testament church at all. The desire for surface stimulation is a sure mark of the fallen nature, the very thing Christ died to deliver us from. Because we are not truly worshippers, we spend a lot of time in the churches just spinning our wheels, burning the gasoline, making a noise but not getting anywhere. Oh, brother or sister, God calls us to worship, but in many instances we are in entertainment, just running a poor second to the theaters.

Philippians 3:3 says, *"For we are the circumcision, which worship God in the spirit, and rejoice in Christ Jesus, and have no confidence in the flesh."* If we understand true worship, we know that the church should not be designed to have a feel-good service, and the music should not be designed to be feel-good music. The Scottish poet Carlyle said, "Let me make a nation's music, and I care not who makes their laws; I will control that nation." There is something very powerful about music and the way it controls people. It works on the emotions. God seeks *"true worshippers,"* and they can only be redeemed people.

Notice carefully the language of the Bible. Not only does God the Son seek, but also God the Father *"seeketh such to worship him."*

God the Spirit Seeks

How does the Holy Spirit seek? If you have trusted Christ as your Savior, you are indwelt by the Holy Spirit. The moment you ask God to forgive your sin and by faith receive Christ as Savior, the Lord Jesus comes to live in you in the Person of the Holy Spirit. You are indwelt forever by the Holy Spirit.

What does God the Spirit do in you? God the Spirit, in the life of the believer, seeks to worship the Lord Jesus and to exalt Christ. This is why the Holy Spirit in us is grieved when we hear something that is not Christ-honoring. God the Spirit is seeking to adore and worship the Lord Jesus Christ.

John 4:24 says, *"God is a Spirit: and they that worship him must worship him in spirit and in truth."* This is a must. The Bible says *"must worship."* There are three "musts" closely gathered in this gospel record. In John 3:7 the Bible says, *"Marvel not that I said unto thee, Ye must be born again."* In John 3:14 the Bible says, *"Even so must the Son of man be lifted up."* The third must is found here in John 4:24, *"God is a Spirit: and they that worship him must worship him in spirit and in truth."* Give great attention to these things.

The Bible tells us in John 4:25, *"The woman saith unto him, I know that Messias cometh, which is called Christ: when he is come, he will tell us all things."* She was opening up her life and was ready to receive Christ. She said, *"I know that Messias cometh."* She was ready to have Christ revealed to her.

We find salvation in verse twenty-six, *"Jesus saith unto her, I that speak unto thee am he."* In other words, the moment she was ready to receive Him, Christ revealed Himself to her. This is the way salvation always comes.

If we are speaking to an unsaved person, we are trying to help him understand the gift of God and who it is that gives this gift. We must talk about who Jesus Christ is and what He promised to do.The need for salvation is recognized through the convicting work done by the Holy Spirit concerning the matter of sin. The moment that person is ready to have Christ revealed to him, then God reveals Himself to that person. In salvation he trusts Christ as Savior, and God makes Himself known to him. This is a work of the Holy Spirit. The Holy Spirit then comes to live in that person. He is redeemed, and now the Spirit of God in him seeks to exalt, adore, and worship the Lord Jesus. This is vital and must be understood to understand worship. This is not worship in soul. This is worship in spirit.

When God made us, He made us spirit, soul, and body. In my spirit I have a conscience. The Bible calls my spirit *"the candle of the Lord"* (Proverbs 20:27). When I trusted Jesus Christ as my Savior, the Lord Jesus came to live in me–in my spirit. This is where God dwells. I must worship God in spirit.

When we speak of music that honors God and is used to bring us into worship of the Lord, we are not talking about soul music, but rather spirit music. This is music that exalts Christ by truthful words. We worship God in our spirit.

There are many people who get emotionally worked up in their souls but do not worship God. They may experience a tremendous high, an exuberance, and an adrenaline rush. People can be moved, stirred, and led emotionally by music. But the Bible says that we are to worship God in spirit.

The Bible says we must worship God *"in spirit and in truth."* Truth is communicated in words. This is why hymn arrangements and other familiar songs are played as the offering is received in our church. The words of the familiar tune are rehearsed in the minds of the hearers and God is exalted. Some churches have elaborate musical presentations but no truth is communicated, no truthful words are rehearsed in the minds of the hearers. The only praise is given to the "performers" for the beautiful performance.

If you want an idea about a true worship service, review Revelation chapter five. God removes the veil and lets us look into heaven and see the Lord worshipped. You should note that in this scene, all eyes are on the Lamb. All eyes are not on the angels, the cherubim, the redeemed, the precious stones, the street of gold, or the gates of pearl. All eyes are on the Lamb!

We may have beautiful buildings, but all eyes must be on the Lamb. We may have people that God has gifted with talent, but all eyes must be on the Lamb. If we are truly going to worship God, all eyes must be on the Lamb. Worship is not a performance. We are to minister to the Lord, and all eyes must be on the Lamb if we are going to be true worshippers.

Revelation 5:9-14 tells us,

> *And they sung a new song, saying, Thou art worthy to take the book, and to open the seals thereof: for thou wast slain, and hast redeemed us to God by thy blood out of every kindred, and tongue, and people, and nation; and hast made us unto our God kings and priests: and we shall reign on the earth. And I beheld, and I heard the voice of many angels round about the throne and the beasts and the elders: and the number of them was ten thousand times ten thousand, and thousands of thousands; saying with a loud voice, Worthy is the Lamb that was slain to receive power, and riches, and wisdom, and strength, and honour, and glory, and blessing. And every creature which is in heaven, and on the earth, and under the earth, and such as are in the sea, and all that are in them, heard*

> *I saying, Blessing, and honour, and glory, and power, be unto him that sitteth upon the throne, and unto the Lamb for ever and ever. And the four beasts said, Amen. And the four and twenty elders fell down and worshipped him that liveth for ever and ever.*

In other words, all eyes were on the Lamb of God, the Lord Jesus Christ. Eyes were not on a praise band, a choir, a soloist, or a preacher. All eyes were on Him. This is true worship.

The preaching and the singing are not the worship. It is only as we look to Christ that we are able to worship our God *"in spirit and in truth."*

So many people are attending meetings and having religious experiences. Their souls are being moved, but their spirits are starving. The adrenaline is running high and the experience is one of exuberance, but their spirits are starving. God must be worshipped *"in spirit and in truth."*

God the Son seeks, God the Father seeks, and God the Holy Spirit seeks. Once the Holy Spirit comes to indwell us, He seeks in us to worship and adore the Lord Jesus Christ.

When we come to the church building and gather together, what should be happening? Our worship begins before we ever arrive in the place that has been set aside for worship. By the way, I am happy that we have a place set aside for our church to come together. This is why we do not allow certain things to be done in this place that has been sanctified as a place of worship. It is not a carnival place or a clowning place. It is not a race track or an entertainment center. It is not a stage. Our services are not productions. This is a place that we have built to come together to honor and adore the Lord. It is set apart as a place where God's people meet together to exalt Christ. It is a place where we can be true worshippers of the true and living God, worshipping Him in spirit and in truth. My heart breaks to think of so many places that have traded true worship for some type of theatrical experience that is starving the spirits of those who come to those places.

There are times when our public meetings or "church services" become substitutes for the true worship we should have. Of course, there are many people who attend the meetings who never truly worship the Lord.

In our homes we should be thinking, "We're going to meet with God and God's people." When we arrive, we arrive at a place where certain things are laid aside. Thoughts have been yielded to Christ. Conversations that we might have in our business dealings are not to be brought into this place because we come to worship the Lord. As we enter in, we find a seat in this place set aside to worship Him.

There may be noise and commotion for a time while we are finding our seats. However, in a few moments, music begins. The music should be music that exalts Christ, not as if we were going out to a ball game. The music should be something that says, "Be still, my soul. We are coming into the presence of God." The music is not given simply so that people will have the noise of their conversation covered. After a moment of hearing that music, we realize that we are coming together to worship God with reverence. We should bow our unworthy heads before the Lord and begin to pray that God will speak to us and deal with us. We want to be true worshippers.

The people who have a part in leading the service do not do it for other people; they do it for God. Those who lead have prepared for the Lord.

Not only does the preacher need to be prepared in prayer, but everyone who has a part in the service needs to be prepared in prayer. Any person who has a part in serving and working should have already prayed and entered into communion with God when he takes his particular place in the worship service. All who have come to worship the Lord need to be praying, believing God, trusting in

God, leaning on God, and expecting Him to move and work. Do not get the idea that we are to have some dead, quiet, lifeless meeting. No! This meeting is very much alive; it is not alive with fleshly entertainment, but alive with the Spirit of the living God.

There are thousands of churches across our land that never have true worship because they have been betrayed by preachers who have turned from being preachers to performers. Some people are no longer singers; they are entertainers. May God help us. A generation has sold out. Let us be true worshippers of the living God.

In my reading, I came across a story about Martin Lloyd Jones, a well-known preacher who is now in heaven. After Martin Jones' death, another preacher went to see his widow and said, "We're going to miss your husband's preaching."

Jones' widow replied, "You're going to miss his preaching, but I'm going to miss his praying. He was mightier in prayer than he was in the pulpit."

When I read that, my heart was so smitten with conviction. I know my wife could not say that; but I want her, by God's grace, to be able to say that.

What we do in public is to no avail if what we are in private is not mighty with God. What so many of us need to do is bring the private, secret part of our lives to the feet of Jesus Christ and say, "Lord Jesus, make me right and holy. Bless me here in the private, secret place of my life." Only then will we be true worshippers of the living God.

IX

The Preacher in the First Century Church

ur confidence is in the Lord and in His Word, not in what we can do. I have made a deliberate choice to place myself under the authority of God's Word. I am grateful to be called to preach. This is God's calling on my life. The Lord has called me to preach His Word.

It has been my experience through the years of serving the Lord that either you pastor a church or you help someone pastor a church. There is more to pastoring a church than preaching; but preaching is certainly a vital part of being a pastor.

Every preacher should have teaching in his preaching, but all teaching is not preaching. Preaching is heralding forth the Word of God. We must recognize that God uses preaching to do so many things in accomplishing His work. We must use and never abuse the power of the pulpit.

What we find in Acts chapter eighteen is a glimpse into the life of the New Testament preacher. The Bible says in Acts 18:24-28,

> *And a certain Jew named Apollos, born at Alexandria, an eloquent man, and mighty in the scriptures, came to Ephesus. This man was instructed in the way of the Lord; and being fervent in the spirit, he spake and taught diligently the things of the Lord, knowing only the baptism of John. And he began to speak boldly in the synagogue: whom when Aquila and Priscilla had heard, they took him unto them, and expounded unto him the way of God more perfectly. And when he was disposed to pass into Achaia, the brethren wrote, exhorting the disciples to receive him: who, when he was come, helped them much which had believed through grace: for he mightily convinced the Jews, and that publicly, showing by the scriptures that Jesus was Christ.*

Consider what the apostle Paul gave as a charge in his closing word in II Timothy 4:1-5,

> *I charge thee therefore before God, and the Lord Jesus Christ, who shall judge the quick and the dead at his appearing and his kingdom; preach the word; be instant in season, out of season; reprove, rebuke, exhort with all longsuffering and doctrine. For the time will come when they will not endure sound doctrine; but after their own lusts shall they heap to themselves teachers, having itching ears; and they shall turn away their ears from the truth, and shall be turned unto fables. But watch thou in all things, endure afflictions, do the work of an evangelist, make full proof of thy ministry.*

We must have a return to Bible preaching. We will be greatly helped by a renewed emphasis on the first century preacher.

I can remember as a young fellow knowing that God was dealing with me. I was a Christian. I had asked God to forgive my sin and by faith I had trusted Christ as my Savior. I had yielded my life to His control to do whatever the Lord wanted me to do. I wanted my life to count for Christ.

I attended a meeting to hear a preacher by the name of Dr. C. E. Autrey. He was a mighty preacher of the Word of God. I was so young, and I thought he was so old. The man seemed ancient to me. I am sure he had reached sixty! He preached with the fervor of a fellow in his twenties. I knew he was well educated. I learned later that he had an earned doctor's degree; yet, he preached simple messages full of the Bible. He preached messages on "Hell," on "Prepare to Meet Thy God," on the word "Lost." He preached a message entitled "The Perils of Postponing God." I listened intently as he would mount the pulpit, stand on his toes, swing his arms, fan the air, raise his voice, hold up the Bible, and declare, *"Thus saith the Lord."*

I thought, "That man is a preacher, and if I were ever a preacher, that is the kind of preacher I want to be." Everything reproduces after its own kind.

We must use and never abuse the power of the pulpit.

The Lord was already dealing with me about what to do with my life and I thought, "I believe God wants me to be a preacher." I had talked a little about it. But I thought doctors had sons that became doctors, and lawyers had sons that became lawyers, and preachers had sons that became preachers. My father was a professional gambler. It was not going to work out for me to be a preacher. But I had this stirring in my heart to declare God's Word, to be God's servant, to speak for the Lord.

Chapter Nine

Night after night as I attended that meeting, God continued to deal with me. I came to a Bible verse in Philippians 2:13 that said, *"For it is God which worketh in you both to will and to do of his good pleasure."* God not only tells us what we are to do with our lives, He gives us desire.

God not only points us in the direction in which we are to go, He gives us the desire to go there. The miracle of the ministry is not that I am in it; the miracle of the ministry is that I have a desire in my heart to be in it. God has placed me in the ministry. This is what the Lord has given me to do. I have a desire to preach His Word.

The miracle of the ministry is not that I am in it; the miracle of the ministry is that I have a desire in my heart to be in it. God has placed me in the ministry.

Later, the Lord led me to pastor a church. God tells us things in His Word about preaching that we need to be aware of as we confront an unbelieving world. The Bible says in I Corinthians 1:18, *"For the preaching of the cross is to them that perish foolishness; but unto us which are saved it is the power of God."*

The preaching of the cross is foolishness to the world. When Paul came to Corinth, he did not say, "I'm going to deal with you on some academic basis." Paul said, *"For I determined not to know any thing among you, save Jesus Christ, and him crucified"* (I Corinthians 2:3).

People are spiritual beings, and we need to declare to them spiritual truth and allow the Spirit of God to deal with their hearts. If God has never called you to preach, you should have an appreciation for anyone that is a God-called preacher.

Charles Haddon Spurgeon said concerning God's calling and the calling of preachers,

> Every Christian is called to spread the gospel. The propagation of the gospel is left, not to a few, but to all the disciples of the Lord Jesus Christ, according to the measure of grace entrusted to them by the Holy Spirit. Each man is bound to minister in his day and generation, both to the church and among unbelievers.
>
> Preachers are not made, they are called. The life of the preacher is not one of choosing, but one of calling. There is no such thing as a preacher not called of God. The un-called may claim the title of preacher, but they are really a speaker speaking man's powerless message.
>
> One called to preach should be able to do nothing else. The first sign of the heavenly call is an intense, all-absorbing desire for the work. In order for there to be a true call to the ministry there must be an irresistible, overwhelming craving and raging thirst for telling to others what God has done for our own souls. One called to preach should be able to stand and proclaim the message God has given him.
>
> Combined with the earnest desire to become a pastor, there must be aptness to teach and some measure of the other qualities needful for the office of a public instructor. In order for a man to prove his call, he must make a successful trial of these.
>
> In order to further prove a man's call, after a little exercise of his gifts, such as I have already spoken

of, he must see a measure of conversion-work going on under his efforts, or he may conclude that he has made a mistake, and, therefore, may go back by the best way he can. The preacher called of God who is preaching God's message will see results, not as a result of his efforts to be a great speaker, but due to the power in God's message. God's Word will not return void.

A step beyond all this is needful in our inquiry. The will of the Lord concerning pastors is made known through the prayerful judgment of His church. It is needful as a proof of your vocation that your preaching should be acceptable to the people of God. Your ability to preach God's Word will be noticed by other Christians.

Whether you value the verdict of the church or not, one thing is certain, that none of you can be pastors without the loving consent of the flock; therefore this will be to you a practical indicator, if not a correct one. If your call from the Lord be a real one, you will not long be silent. As surely as the man wants his hour, so surely the hour wants its man.

Do not run about inviting yourselves to preach here and there. Be more concerned about your ability than your opportunity, and more earnest about your walk with God than about either. The sheep will know the God-sent shepherd; the porter of the fold will open to you, and the flock will know your voice.

Develop an appreciation for preachers of God's Word. We should honor all men as God's Word says. When we think about what God is doing in the lives of people, when you think about God calling people to preach, it is a serious thing.

I say to young men, "When you're going to announce God has called you to preach, remember that announcement will follow you all of your life. If you vary from it, if you move off course, someone is going to say to you, 'I thought years ago you were called of God to preach.'"

There are many people who have no respect for God, no respect for the things of God, and no respect for the people of God. May God help us to have the right attitude toward the things of God and toward people God has called to preach.

The First Century Preacher Was Persuasive

The Bible tells us of the apostle Paul and his preaching in Acts 18:13, *"Saying, This fellow persuadeth men to worship God contrary to the law."* This shows us so much about Paul's preaching. He was a persuader.

Our preaching should be persuasive. We should not try to castigate people or be harsh with people, but when you hear a God-called man preach, there should be persuasiveness in his preaching. That is the New Testament pattern.

The First Century Preacher Warned in His Preaching

In Acts 20:31 the apostle Paul himself said, *"Therefore watch, and remember, that by the space of three years I ceased not to warn every one night and day with tears."* He warned people in his preaching.

Sounding a warning alarms people. When there is war going on in certain parts of the world, they sound a siren letting people know bombs are approaching or missiles are approaching. People are alarmed. They prepare. The warning is sounded.

A God-called preacher, if he is following the New Testament pattern, will warn people in his preaching. He will speak to them about the terror of the Lord. He will speak to them about the certain judgment of God. He will preach to them about the certainty of hell if one dies without Christ. He will say things in a sermon that may not even be said to a person face to face in such a way as to declare this clear warning.

The First Century Preacher Reasoned in His Preaching

In Acts 24:25 the Bible says of Paul's preaching, *"And as he reasoned of righteousness, temperance, and judgment to come, Felix trembled, and answered, Go thy way for this time; when I have a convenient season, I will call for thee."* Paul reasoned in his preaching.

I do not think one could qualify New Testament preaching as the flimsy preaching that people hear so much of today, simply saying, "You need to trust the Lord." Salvation is talked about with cute clichés. The New Testament preacher is a man who takes the Word of God and reasons with people. He shows them the Scripture. He deals logically with the truth of God's Word. He presses the matter. He deals with the subject of sin.

The Bible says Paul reasoned with them–*"And as he reasoned of righteousness, temperance, and judgment to come."* This was not some speech Paul got through in a hurry. This was a heartfelt, persuasive warning. Paul reasoned with them. He declared the truth.

Concerning Paul's preaching, the Bible says in Acts 28:23,

> *And when they had appointed him a day, there came many to him into his lodging; to whom he expounded and testified the kingdom of God, persuading them concerning Jesus, both out of the law of Moses, and out of the prophets, from morning till evening.*

Paul was everlastingly at it, expounding the Word of God. He logically dealt with the great subjects of Christ, sin, and the only way of salvation.

The First Century Preacher Preached in the Power of the Holy Spirit

If we had no one else to examine but the apostle Paul, we would find certain things to be true. Paul put forth the truth of God in logical form. He preached in the power of the Holy Spirit. In I Thessalonians 1:5 Paul tells us, *"For our gospel came not unto you in word only, but also in power, and in the Holy Ghost."* He preached in power.

Paul pressed for a verdict. The preacher must be very careful here because he is not the person who gives thumbs up or thumbs down about God and salvation. Unfortunately, when some men stand in the pulpit, they behave as if they can decide who will be saved and who will not be saved. We must be careful about how we give the gospel invitation so that it is not of men. We must recognize the work of God, because *"salvation is of the LORD"* (Jonah 2:9).

We can freely declare the truth that the salvation offered is offered to all who will come because the Lord has tasted death for every man, but the Spirit of God must draw a man. And the New Testament preacher must recognize that it must be God's Spirit dealing with a man, convicting that man of his sin in order that he might repent of his sin and put his faith in Christ for salvation. Yet he presses for that verdict. He brings people to see the truth and helps them recognize that they must reach that verdict. He is dependent on the Holy Spirit. He has no confidence in the flesh.

The First Century Preacher Was Mighty in the Scriptures

If we were going to take a model for New Testament preaching, there is no greater model than Jesus Christ. Prayerfully read the discourses of Christ. Examine His preaching given at the end of this chapter.

There is also so very much about preaching in the first century church revealed to us in the life of Apollos. Let us study some of the wonderful things God says concerning him. The Bible says in Acts 18:24, *"And a certain Jew named Apollos, born at Alexandria, an eloquent man...."*

Alexandria was a place of learning. The world's most famous library was once located there. Apollos was an eloquent man, called by many who study the Bible the most eloquent of all New Testament preachers. But I submit that his power, his usefulness, was not in his eloquence. God tells us about this New Testament preacher. He says of Apollos that he was *"mighty in the scriptures."*

People who have studied the life of the evangelist D. L. Moody will tell you that Moody was an uneducated man who left home as a young man because his family was so poor that his mother could not feed him. He traveled to Boston, then on to Chicago. Moody became a mighty man of God. The thing that characterized the life and ministry of Moody was his knowledge of Scripture. He knew the Word of God.

I do not believe one can be a New Testament preacher without striving to be mighty in the Scriptures, to know the Word of God, to preach the Word of God, and to declare the Word of God. It is the Word of God that is *"quick, and powerful, and sharper than any twoedged sword"* (Hebrews 4:12).

As a very young man, I walked into my pastor's study and asked him if I might borrow some of his sermon books. He said, "Take any of them you wish to take and read them and preach the sermons. I've preached them all."

As I loaded my arms with books and started out of his study, he said to me as I was near the door, "Let me tell you something, Clarence, before you go. If you learn to preach the Bible, you'll never run out of anything to preach." I have never forgotten what he said. "If you learn to preach the Bible, you'll never run out of anything to preach." That was great advice.

In my own life I have seen times when God threw a rope from heaven in the form of a verse of Scripture or a passage of Scripture. It was heaven's rope extended to me to grab hold and say, "Hold on. It's going to be rough for a while, but you're going to make it. God's Word is going to see you through." Oh, the power of His Word!

The Bible says this first century preacher was *"mighty in the scriptures."* All of us need to strive to have a knowledge of God's Word. We study the Word of God in order to obey God's Word, not simply to know it as some academic achievement. I am convinced that God will teach His Word by His blessed Holy Spirit. If we intend to obey His Word, He will teach us His Word.

Apollos was a preacher. He was eloquent. He was from Alexandria, a place of learning identified with people who were in "the know." He came to Ephesus. He did not come from Alexandria to Ephesus simply as an eloquent man; he came preaching *"mighty in the scriptures."* Every preacher needs to strive to be mighty in the Scriptures.

The First Century Preacher Was Instructed in the Way of the Lord

The Bible says of Apollos in Acts 18:25, *"This man was instructed in the way of the Lord...."* This means he submitted himself to be instructed. Instruction has to do with knowing things and being able to get hold of things with the eventual purpose of giving those things to other people, teaching something that was formerly unknown.

Apollos was an eloquent man and no doubt an educated man. He placed himself in a position of a student to be instructed in the things of the Lord. Every preacher should be one who is learning, studying, applying what he has learned, and growing in the Lord.

It is unfortunate to see so many talented young preachers never grow as they should. Like Apollos, every preacher must submit himself to be instructed in the way of the Lord.

The First Century Preacher Was Fervent in the Spirit

The Bible says in Acts 18:25, *"...and being fervent in the spirit...."* I have prayed with men who were fervent in prayer. It changed my thinking about prayer. I had been so tentative in prayer. The Bible says we should be fervent in spirit.

The Bible says Apollos was *"fervent in the spirit."* There was a fervency about him. There is a great difference between a man preaching with fervency and not preaching with fervency. There is a difference between listening to a man who believes what he is saying and listening to a fellow who has doubts about what he is saying. This New Testament preacher was fervent in the spirit.

The First Century Preacher Was Diligent

The Bible continues describing Apollos, saying, *"...he spake and taught diligently the things of the Lord...."*

I remember reading years ago an illustration given by W. B. Riley about diligence. He said the best example he had ever seen of diligence was a shoe-shine man. Dr. Riley declared, "I took my seat and I put my shoe on the stand for the man to shine it. He never looked up. He just stayed at it. He worked at that shoe and then he worked at the other shoe. He never looked up. He never raised his head. He didn't do anything but work on those shoes until he finished those shoes." He said, "He was diligent."

The Bible says Apollos was diligent. He made this his life's work. He was giving himself to it. The man who is a preacher of the gospel should be a man who is diligent. Apollos *"spake and taught diligently the things of the Lord."*

The First Century Preacher Was Bold

The Bible continues, *"...knowing only the baptism of John. And he began to speak boldly in the synagogue...."* Apollos hit a little bump in the road. He was teaching and preaching everything he knew. He began to speak boldly.

Boldness may sometimes come across as arrogance, but only if it lacks humility. Our confidence is in the Lord, and sometimes people who are not confident in the Lord mistake someone who is for being arrogant. The boldness we need grows out of our faith and confidence in the Lord.

Boldness may sometimes come across as arrogance, but only if it lacks humility.

The apostle Paul had spent about a year and a half with Aquila and Priscilla; no doubt, he taught them. When they heard Apollos preaching boldly but only knowing the baptism of John, the Bible says in Acts 18:26, "*Whom when Aquila and Priscilla had heard, they took him unto them, and expounded unto him the way of God more perfectly.*" Is that not a precious statement?

They were tender and loving. They literally walked him through this. They joined themselves to him. They had in mind all along that this man was going to be mightily used of God and they were going to do what God had for them to do in encouraging this preacher.

God's people can help God's man if they have the Spirit of God to do it. Here was a couple trained and nurtured by the apostle Paul, who put their arms around Apollos and helped him. The Bible says in verses twenty-six and twenty-seven,

> *They took him unto them, and expounded unto him the way of God more perfectly. And when he was disposed to pass into Achaia, the brethren wrote, exhorting the disciples to receive him: who, when he was come, helped them much which had believed through grace.*

Why do you think Apollos was able to help them? It was because he had been helped by Aquila and Priscilla.

People say, "If we'd just get the right preacher, we'd have a great church." Many a right preacher has never had the right people with whom to work. It has to be a marriage between pastor and people.

The First Century Preacher Mightily Convinced Concerning Christ

The Bible says in Acts 18:28, *"For he mightily convinced the Jews...."* Apollos was mighty in the Scriptures, but just going so far as John's baptism. But now he was going to deal with the Jews concerning the deity of Jesus Christ. He was able to do that because Aquila and Priscilla took him aside. He mightily convinced the Jews.

The word *"mightily"* means "well stretched; carefully put together as many pearls on a string." Apollos took the Scriptures and placed them on a logical string and mightily convinced the Jews concerning Christ.

The First Century Preacher Declared Publicly That Jesus Is Christ

The Bible says, *"...and that publicly, showing by the scriptures that Jesus was Christ."* You cannot have a public ministry if your private life is not what it should be. You can try, but the power of the preacher is not in his public speaking. God does not bless and use a man for what he is in public. You may be enamored by someone's public ability, but God does not bless and use that man because of what he is in public. The Lord looks at a man's heart. The New Testament preacher declared the message of Jesus Christ publicly, but he asked God to help him keep his heart right privately.

Discourses of the Lord Jesus Christ

Major Discourses:

1. The So-Called Sermon on the Mount (Matthew 5,6,7).
2. His Instructions to the Twelve Apostles (Matthew 10).
3. John the Baptist and His Mission (Matthew 11).
4. Satan Casting out Satan, Holy Spirit, etc... (Matthew 12:22-50).
5. Parables of the Kingdom of Heaven (Matthew 13).
6. The Externals and Internals of Godliness (Matthew 15:1-20).
7. The Confession and Knowledge of Christ (Matthew 16:13-28).
8. The Magnitude of Small Numbers (Matthew 18:1-20).
9. The True Nature and Patience of Forgiveness (Matthew 18:21-35).
10. The Danger and Destructiveness of Avarice (Matthew 19:16; 20:16).
11. The Peril and Meanness of Ambition (Matthew 20:20-38).
12. Obedience and Disobedience to Divine Authority (Matthew 21:23-44).

13. The Call and the Chosen of God (Matthew 22:1-14).
14. The Guilt and Condemnation of Hypocrisy (Matthew 23).
15. The Signs of Christ's Coming and the End (Matthew 24, 25).
16. The Vineyard and Unfaithful Husbandmen (Mark 12:1-12).
17. The Sermon in the Synagogue at Nazareth (Luke 4:16-30).
18. The Love that Is Born of Forgiveness (Luke 7:37-50).
19. Six Wrong Tempers: Intolerance, Ambition, Revenge, etc... (Luke 9:43-62).
20. The Commission of the Seventy (Luke 10:1-24).
21. The Good Samaritan and Love to Neighbor (Luke 10:25-42).
22. The Lesson of Importunity in Prayer (Luke 11:1-13).
23. The Sin and Folly of Covetousness (Luke 12:13-59).
24. The Strait Gate and the Shut Door (Luke 13:23-35).
25. The Feast and the Guests (Luke 14:7-35).
26. The Love of God for the Lost (Luke 15).
27. The Responsibility of Stewardship (Luke 16:1-31).
28. Conditions of Prevailing Prayer (Luke 18:1-14).
29. The Nobleman and His Servants (Luke 19:1-27).
30. The Rebuke of the Sadducees (Luke 20:27-47).
31. The Post-Resurrection Exposition (Luke 24:13-34).
32. The New Birth and Eternal Life (John 3).
33. The Water that Quenches Thirst (John 4:1-42).
34. The Divine Equality and Authority of the Son (John 5:17-47).

35. The Bread Which Is from Heaven (John 6:26-71).

36. The Two Fatherhoods, God and Devil (John 8:21-59).

37. The Good Shepherd and the Sheep (John 10:1-38).

38. The Humility of True Service (John 13:1-20).

39. The Great Preparatory Discourse (John 14-16).

40. The Intercessory Prayer (John 17).

Minor Discourses:

1. The True Law of the Sabbath Rest (Matthew 12:1-13).
2. The Leaven of the Pharisees (Matthew 16:1-12).
3. Divorce and Marital Relations (Matthew 19:3-12).
4. The Moral Meaning of His Miracles (Mark 2:3-17).
5. The Vice of Intolerance and Bigotry (Mark 9:38-50).
6. The Resurrection Life and Its Conditions (Mark 12:18-37).
7. The First and Greatest Commandment (Mark 12:28-34).
8. God's Estimate of Human Gifts (Mark 12:41-44).
9. The Last Great Command and Commission (Mark 16:14-20).
10. The Barren Fig Tree and Its Lesson (Luke 13:1-9).
11. Offenses and the Forgiving Spirit (Luke 17:1-10).
12. The Address on the Last Day of Feast (John 7:37-39).
13. The Light of the World (John 8:12-20).
14. The Resurrection, Spiritual and Physical (John 11:25, 26).
15. The Corn of Wheat and the Crop (John 12:21-36).
16. Believing and Rejecting (John 12:42-50).

X

The Vision of the First Century Church

The book of Acts provides a true record of the first century church. It is also the book of the continuing work of Christ in the Person of the Holy Spirit. The lives of those who followed the Lord Jesus provide examples for us to follow. The human penman for the book of Acts was Luke, the companion of the apostle Paul. He penned the account of Paul giving his testimony in great detail in the twenty-sixth chapter of Acts.

Paul had been arrested and taken to Caesarea, a beautiful seacoast city. He had gone before one ruler, Felix, and then before Festus. After Festus heard Paul, Agrippa II arrived in Caesarea with his sister, Bernice. Immediately, he heard about this prisoner and the uproar that had been caused because of the controversy surrounding his life and ministry. Agrippa II desired to hear Paul.

On a certain day, with all the pomp and splendor of a king, Agrippa and his sister Bernice, along with Festus and the chief captains and principal men of the city, met together in a large area. As they gathered, Paul was brought in the room to stand before them. Festus turned to the king and said, "This is the man about whom I have been telling you! This is the circumstance surrounding his life." The king turned to Paul and said, *"Thou art permitted to speak for thyself."* In Acts chapter twenty-six Paul began to speak. We read in Acts 26:1-29,

> *I think myself happy, king Agrippa, because I shall answer for myself this day before thee touching all the things whereof I am accused of the Jews: especially because I know thee to be expert in all customs and questions which are among the Jews: wherefore I beseech thee to hear me patiently.*
>
> *My manner of life from my youth, which was at the first among mine own nation at Jerusalem, know all the Jews; which knew me from the beginning, if they would testify, that after the most straitest sect of our religion I lived a Pharisee. And now I stand and am judged for the hope of the promise made of God unto our fathers: unto which promise our twelve tribes, instantly serving God day and night, hope to come. For which hope's sake, king Agrippa, I am accused of the Jews.*
>
> *Why should it be thought a thing incredible with you, that God should raise the dead? I verily thought with myself, that I ought to do many things contrary to the name of Jesus of Nazareth. Which thing I also did in Jerusalem: and many of the saints did I shut up in prison, having received authority from the chief priests; and when they were put to death, I gave my voice against them. And I punished them oft in every synagogue, and compelled them to blaspheme; and being exceedingly mad against them, I persecuted them even unto strange cities. Whereupon as I went*

to Damascus with authority and commission from the chief priests, at midday, O king, I saw in the way a light from heaven, above the brightness of the sun, shining round about me and them which journeyed with me. And when we were all fallen to the earth, I heard a voice speaking unto me, and saying in the Hebrew tongue, Saul, Saul, why persecutest thou me? it is hard for thee to kick against the pricks. And I said, Who art thou, Lord? And he said, I am Jesus whom thou persecutest. But rise, and stand upon thy feet: for I have appeared unto thee for this purpose, to make thee a minister and a witness both of these things which thou hast seen, and of those things in the which I will appear unto thee; delivering thee from the people, and from the Gentiles, unto whom now I send thee, to open their eyes, and to turn them from darkness to light, and from the power of Satan unto God, that they may receive forgiveness of sins, and inheritance among them which are sanctified by faith that is in me.

Whereupon, O king Agrippa, I was not disobedient unto the heavenly vision: but shewed first unto them of Damascus, and at Jerusalem, and throughout all the coasts of Judaea, and then to the Gentiles, that they should repent and turn to God, and do works meet for repentance. For these causes the Jews caught me in the temple, and went about to kill me. Having therefore obtained help of God, I continue unto this day, witnessing both to small and great, saying none other things than those which the prophets and Moses did say should come: that Christ should suffer, and that he should be the first that should rise from the dead, and should shew light unto the people, and to the Gentiles.

Chapter Ten

And as he thus spake for himself, Festus said with a loud voice, Paul, thou art beside thyself; much learning doth make thee mad. But he said, I am not mad, most noble Festus; but speak forth the words of truth and soberness. For the king knoweth of these things, before whom also I speak freely: for I am persuaded that none of these things are hidden from him; for this thing was not done in a corner.

King Agrippa, believest thou the prophets? I know that thou believest. Then Agrippa said unto Paul, Almost thou persuadest me to be a Christian. And Paul said, I would to God, that not only thou, but also all that hear me this day, were both almost, and altogether such as I am, except these bonds.

Give special attention to the expression Paul declared to King Agrippa, *"I was not disobedient unto the heavenly vision."* Paul hinged all his behavior on this *"heavenly vision."* What tremendous insight we find here concerning the first century church!

Becoming a first century church should be the goal of every church. Most churches are caught up in the "fads" that are available. We must stay with the Bible. We recognize that God's Word will not return void. The strongest, most helpful thing done in the ministry is to give forth the Word of God line upon line, precept upon precept, as we teach and preach the Bible.

As we look at the vision of the first century church, we learn that out of our vision, everything else will come. If our vision is not right, then nothing else is right. As a matter of fact, it is easier to be in "church work" without vision than it is to be in a church with vision. I mean by this that if we are without vision, then we simply do what we want to do. We do what we think is best using the ideas we think people will approve of, things that will "work" in our thinking.

But if our vision truly comes from God, it is a different matter altogether. Everything begins with God. The clearer our vision of God, the clearer everything else in life will be. Everything rises or falls on leadership, and leadership rises or falls on our vision of God.

We can learn so very much about this matter of vision from the powerful Old Testament account in Isaiah chapter six where the Bible says,

> *In the year that king Uzziah died I saw also the Lord sitting upon a throne, high and lifted up, and his train filled the temple. Above it stood the seraphims: each one had six wings; with twain he covered his face, and with twain he covered his feet, and with twain he did fly. And one cried unto another, and said, Holy, holy, holy, is the* LORD *of hosts: the whole earth is full of his glory. And the posts of the door moved at the voice of him that cried, and the house was filled with smoke. Then said I, Woe is me! for I am undone; because I am a man of unclean lips, and I dwell in the midst of a people of unclean lips: for mine eyes have seen the King, the Lord of hosts. Then flew one of the seraphims unto me, having a live coal in his hand, which he had taken with the tongs from off the altar: and he laid it upon my mouth, and said, Lo, this hath touched thy lips; and thine iniquity is taken away, and thy sin purged. Also I heard the voice of the Lord, saying, Whom shall I send, and who will go for us? Then said I, Here am I; send me.*

Isaiah saw the Lord high and lifted up! Remember, our vision of God determines everything else we are going to do! It not only determines everything we are going to do; it determines the way we attempt to accomplish it. The clearer our vision of God, the clearer everything else becomes in life. As a matter of fact, the Bible says in Proverbs 29:18, *"Where there is no vision, the people perish."*

Do you believe some people have seen things that others have not seen? Is it possible that some believers have seen what other Christians have not seen? Yes.

Where are the New Testament Christians today? Where is the Christian faith that we find so freely spoken of in the Bible? Where is the faith of those first century Christians? This matter is all connected to the vision of the first century church.

> *The clearer our vision of God, the clearer everything else in life will be. Everything rises or falls on leadership, and leadership rises or falls on our vision of God.*

When the Lord Jesus came to this earth, He came to bleed and die for our sins. He took on a robe of flesh, and in that body He went to Calvary and paid your sin debt and mine. If it were possible to go to heaven without the death, burial, and resurrection of the Lord Jesus Christ, then it was not necessary for Christ to bleed and die for our sins. If we could work our way to heaven, then why did the Lord Jesus Christ die for our sin? He paid our sin debt because He was the only sinless One. He owed no debt of His own, yet He went to the cross and bled and died for our sin. The billows of God's wrath rolled on the Son of God as He tasted death for every man and became sin for us. He bled and died, was buried, and rose again because there is no other way to God except through the Lord Jesus Christ!

There is no other way! If this is true, then why do so many churches become engaged in everything imaginable other than the work that God has given us to do? The Lord Jesus said, *"As the Father hath sent me, even so send I you."* Vision is a discerning matter. It is a defining matter. It is a refining matter!

As you think of the Lord and see Him in your mind's eye, how do you see Him? Do you see Him as a baby in a manger? Do you see Him hanging on a cross and bleeding and dying? So often, people see Him only in His humiliation and give Him no more than a sympathy vote. Perhaps they shed a tear for Him. The Bible declares in the book of Hebrews that we should see Him high, exalted, and lifted up. In Hebrews 8:1 the Bible says, *"Now of the things which we have spoken this is the sum: We have such an high priest, who is set on the right hand of the throne of the Majesty in the heavens."*

In other words, the sum of the matter is that He came to this earth without ceasing to be God; He became a man without ceasing to be God. He was robed in flesh and dwelt among us. He went to the cross and bled and died for our sins. He owed no sin debt of His own. He died for our sin debt. He was buried in a borrowed tomb, and He arose from the grave alive forevermore. He ascended into heaven where He ever lives to make intercession for us, and He is exalted on high as the God of this universe.

How great is your God? What vision do you have of Him? The reason the first century church was able to accomplish all they accomplished was because of the vision they had of God.

Paul spoke of that vision in Acts chapter twenty-six concerning his salvation. All of his religious endeavors left him lost, without God and without hope. All of your religious endeavors will leave you the same way.

If we have the vision of the first century church, certain things will characterize that vision and will be true of our church. Though we live twenty centuries later, the same things will be true of our church if we have a first century vision of God. We need the vision of the first century church! Leadership in the local church is properly guided by the right vision of God.

This Vision Created Accountability to God

I certainly do not consider myself to be an authority on the ministry, but if I could put my finger on what most Christians fail to do, it would be the failure in the matter of their own personal accountability to God. We must see God for who He truly is, not a small god or a god who is a buddy; not a god who is like a butler coming quickly at our bidding; but the Creator God who spoke the world into existence, the God before whom we shall bow and confess that He is Lord. When we see Him as He truly is, and we enter into His presence, it creates in us accountability to God.

> *Leadership in the local church is properly guided by the right vision of God.*

The lives of most professing Christians are characterized by being forty miles wide and one inch deep. Who motivates you? Who stirs your heart? Who has caught you and captured you?

Listen intently to what Paul said as he stood before King Agrippa. Paul knew something about this man and his illicit relationship with his own sister. He knew certain things about others who were in that room. They came in their pomp and splendor, dressed in their royal gowns, and they brought Paul in to question him. Before long it was the interrogators who were on trial, and it was the Holy Spirit speaking through His man that confronted them.

I would rather have had what Paul had that day than everything they had or ever could have in this world. He had seen the Lord for who He is, and he said before them, *"I was not disobedient unto the heavenly vision."*

Vision means revelation. It is how God reveals Himself to us. Whose vision are we following? The truth is, we should have God's heart in our heart. We should understand something about the heart of God and what God wants to accomplish in this world. We should look at people the way the Lord looks at people.

This vision of God brings us together in our accountability to God. I said to one of our workers recently, a kind, wonderful person, "I want you to back up just a minute. Instead of coming to me with your plans and ideas, I want you to stop long enough, be still, and try to find out what God has put in my heart to do." I dare say that any man or woman leading in a matter who has seen a vision of God and what God wants him or her to do is dealing with the same thing. This vision of God is for all those who know the Lord. It brings us to one great purpose–His purpose.

> *Before long it was the interrogators who were on trial, and it was the Holy Spirit speaking through His man that confronted them.*

Do we have a single purpose? Is there something specific about which we can say, "This is what God has given us to do"? When we see the Lord as Paul saw the Lord high and lifted up, and when we understand the call of God upon our lives knowing that God has changed our lives and forgiven our sin and given us a ministry, and we truly know the Lord for who He is, it creates an accountability in our lives to God and God alone. Vision comes the same way for each believer. It is not a matter of "casting" or "sharing." It is a matter of each individual believer seeking God, praying, and desiring to know God. Our vision of Him will never be in contradiction to His Word.

Because of their vision, those first century Christians could not be stopped. They accomplished what no one else could or did accomplish because of their vision. Their vision was not about things;

it was about being captured by God and His mission. The Lord has a mission in this world. As they got close enough to God to see the Lord and understand the Lord Jesus Christ, then they understood what they were to do with their lives. Our work is to do His work. We are called first and foremost to be *"with him"* (Mark 3:14).

There should be such Christ-likeness among God's people that strangers who come into contact with us sense His presence. So many of us have good intentions and sincerely want to be busy. We think that a good work ethic is a good thing to have, and it is; but there are so many people engaged in work that is not divinely directed. Multitudes have made service their goal and not God. There are so many people spending their lives for something that has not come from their vision of God.

If we are going to be certain about any thing, we need to be certain about this, because we cannot get our lives back once they have been spent. The vision of the first century church created accountability to God and His work in the world.

THIS VISION DEMANDED ACTION

There is no retreat from this! It demands action! Paul said, "When I met the Lord, there was something I had to do!" He told Agrippa in verse nineteen,

> *Whereupon, O king Agrippa, I was not disobedient unto the heavenly vision: but shewed first unto them of Damascus, and at Jerusalem, and throughout all the coasts of Judaea, and then to the Gentiles, that they should repent and turn to God, and do works meet for repentance.*

Immediately Paul began to speak to people about the message God gave him. If a man is truly following the Lord, he is going to want people to know the same Lord he is following! The Lord Jesus Christ said, *"Go ye into all the world, and preach the gospel to every creature"* (Mark 16:15).

When we see the Lord high, exalted, and lifted up, it creates this accountability to God and God alone, and we must do what God has given us to do. We have become witnesses. Because of this we must witness. I do not have to sit around and wonder what the Lord wants me to do. I do not have to try to imagine what the church I am privileged to pastor is supposed to do. I do not have to dream up schemes and plans about ministries we should be engaged in near us and around the world. When we have seen the Lord and know God's heart about the matter, then our hearts are to be in tune with what God has in His heart. Our work is to be wholeheartedly engaged in His work. Get in on what God is doing.

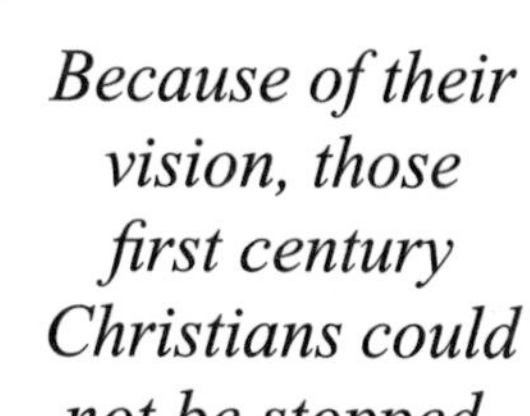

Because of their vision, those first century Christians could not be stopped.

This is exactly what Paul said concerning getting the message of Jesus Christ to all people. They must repent and turn to God and do the works meet for repentance. It is our work to get the gospel out! God is our goal. The task is not the goal. The task comes from our desire to please God and obey Him.

I do not like to think of myself as a driven man. I do not like to think that there is some external force pushing me, driving me, and making me do what I do. There are times in my life when out of sheer duty I must say, "You are going to do what you are supposed to do!" But if I am abiding in the Lord, seeking after God, and doing what He has given me to do, then there is compulsion from within that leads me to take action and speak to people about Christ.

If I am not sensitive and keenly aware that all men are eternal and that they are going to live and die and either go to heaven or hell, if I am not keenly aware that God has put me here to compassionately press the issue of trusting Christ, it is not because I have lost concern for people; it is because I have lost my vision of God and what God is doing in this world. I must get that vision of God clear again.

The Christian life is not a sight life.

Paul followed the Lord's methods and trained others. He did exactly what the Lord Jesus Christ did on this earth, seeking after those who were lost and bringing them to Christ. A church must have a first century vision. That vision is a vision of God. Paul said, *"I was not disobedient unto the heavenly vision."* It creates accountability and demands action.

This Vision Required Faith

There is a great deal of confusion here. Some people assume that the second part, the demand for action, is where great faith is required. Attempting things for God is where action has been demanded. Expecting great things from God, as the missionary William Carey said, is where the faith is required.

God said to Joshua, "Put your feet in the water and I will open the water so you can cross the Jordan!" Because God said, "Put your feet in the water," Joshua put his feet in the water, and God opened the Jordan. His vision of God demanded action, but it also required faith.

God has told us to go into all the world and preach the gospel to every creature. We must take this action, and this action requires faith. It requires faith because we attempt more than we can do. We attempt what we cannot possibly get done in the energy of our flesh. It requires faith because of the opposition it brings. This is what Paul said in testifying, "As soon as I did what God told me to do, the Jews sought to kill me." Opposition and hardship turn many people back. Faith is required for this job!

There is a continual refining process after you are in the process. There is a refining process that is ongoing; it never ceases. If you think that you are going to start out following the Lord, and for a little while God is going to test your faith and refine you, and that will be the end of the refining process, you are wrong. It is going to continue all of your life as long as you are on this earth.

The Christian life is not a sight life. By faith we catch a vision of God. It is a faith life to follow God and do what God wants us to do. It is always going to require faith! When Nehemiah came to rebuild the walls of Jerusalem, the Bible says that before he talked to others about what he was going to do, he communed with God. Nehemiah said, *"So I came to Jerusalem, and was there three days. And I arose in the night, I and some few men with me; neither told I any man what my God had put in my heart to do at Jerusalem: neither was there any beast with me, save the beast that I rode upon"* (Nehemiah 2:11-12).

The Christian life is not a sight life. By faith we catch a vision of God. It is a faith life to follow God and do what God wants us to do.

He said, "I have already caught a vision of God and taken action. I am not telling any man what God put in my heart to do." Then when he started rebuilding the walls, Sanballet and Tobiah started doing everything they could to discourage him and stop him.

He said to them in Nehemiah 6:3, *"And I sent messengers unto them, saying, I am doing a great work, so that I cannot come down: why should the work cease, whilst I leave it, and come down to you?"* In other words, after he followed the Lord and took action, faith was required to stay in it. This is true of all our lives!

What has God assigned to us? This is the thing that is going to keep us on course. This is the thing that is going to help us not to turn back in the day of trouble. This is the thing that is going to keep us strong in the midst of the battle. We must know that God has appointed us to this task.

The day that it does not require faith is the day that it is not Christian living. Paul explained that he was following the Lord. He had committed no crime against the Jews, no crime against the temple, and no crime against Caesar. Following the Lord led him to be incarcerated as a prisoner. As a Roman citizen, he had a right to appeal to Caesar. He was following God by faith.

Paul knew that he was in the center of God's will in jail in Caesarea. Can you imagine such a thing? Can you also imagine the peace of heart that it gave him to know that he was in God's will even though these circumstances had taken place?

Beloved, there is a Christian life that God wants us to live that is so simple. It is as simple as saying, "Lord, what do You want me to do? What are You doing in this world? I want to get in on that!" This may sound like an oversimplification, but if we can discover what God is doing in the world, and be involved in what He is doing, this is all that is required.

Once you see what God is doing, you must take action. Once you see what God is doing and who God is, God is going to hold you accountable and require that you live by faith for the resources to get it accomplished. This is the vision of the first century church.

The God of the first century church is the same God we serve today. He says, *"I am the Lord, I change not"* (Malachi 3:6). If they could have a vision of God in the first century, we can have a vision of the same God. We are accountable to Him.

This vision demands that we take action. All along the journey, it will require faith. When we see our weaknesses and His strength, our inability and His ability, this is what it is all about. I love doing what God has given me to do. I love being where God has placed me.

I must keep this simple; I am His servant, and this is a task that He has assigned me. He demands that I take action and stay at it, and around every turn I am required to exercise faith in Him.

THE MAN OF VISION THE MAN OF AMBITION

"THE BIBLICAL LEADER"	VS.	"THE PRAGMATIST"
Begins with God	vs.	Begins with man
Does a work of faith	vs.	Does a work of sight
Believes, "If it is right; God will bless it."	vs.	Believes, "If it works; it must be right."
Is obedient to God	vs.	Is in competition with others
Desires God to be glorified	vs.	Desires approval of man
Is Christ-centered	vs.	Is man-centered
Serves God	vs.	Serves self
Lives a life of *"simplicity and godly sincerity"* II Corinthians 1:12	vs.	Lives a life of complexity

THESE ARE TWO TOTALLY DIFFERENT WAYS OF LIFE.

XI

The Pioneering Spirit of the First Century Church

he Lord is real to us only as we put our faith in Him. The Christian life is a faith life. Without faith, it is impossible to please God. The Bible says that *"we must believe that he is and that he is a rewarder of them that diligently seek him"* (Hebrews 11:6).

We need to recapture what could be termed the "pioneering spirit" that springs forth from the faith life. As we follow the history of the people of God, we find them being led by Moses toward the Promised Land. After the wilderness wanderings and the death of Moses, Joshua led the Israelites across the Jordan and into Canaan. Battles were fought and victories were won, but the task was not complete. The children of God were to drive out the enemy, but this is something that they did not do.

In the second chapter of the book of Judges, God tells us that after the death of Joshua, there rose up a generation which did not know the Lord or the mighty works which God had done. Again and again, the Bible says that the children of Israel did not drive out the enemy. In Judges 1:21 we read, *"Benjamin did not drive out the Jebusites."* Verse twenty-seven of the same chapter says, *"Neither did Manasseh drive out the inhabitants of Bethshean."*

Verse twenty-nine says, *"Neither did Ephraim drive out the Canaanites that dwelt in Gezer."* Verse thirty says, *"Neither did Zebulun drive out the inhabitants of Kitron."* Verse thirty-one says, *"Neither did Asher drive out the inhabitants of Accho."* Verse thirty-three says, *"Neither did Naphtali drive out the inhabitants of Bethshemesh."*

The faith required to trust God for the complete victory is also the faith that would have made God real to His people.

The faith required to trust God for the complete victory is also the faith that would have made God real to His people. Their refusal to trust God for the victory and their choice to live without faith brought them to the place where God says of their generation, they *"knew not the LORD"* (Judges 2:10).

Men with a pioneering spirit came before them, but their generation was willing to simply rest on those who had gone before. Though this rest was enjoyable and their complacency less of a burden, the absence of faith caused them to lose touch with God. They went by the same name as their forefathers, they lived in the same land as their forefathers, but they did not know firsthand the God of their forefathers.

There have been pioneers who had that "pioneering spirit." They were committed to follow Christ, just as surely as Abraham looked for a city whose builder and maker was God. The pioneers did not know the end of their earthly endeavor. They had enough light only to take the next step of faith. As they trusted God to meet their needs, their needs seemed insurmountable, but God came through; for without God, it would have been impossible.

They could do more than talk about their impossibility; they felt the impossibility. They faced the impossibility. They dealt with the impossibility and cast themselves entirely on the mercy of God. Not only did the Lord provide, He became real to them as they trusted Him to meet their need.

In so many places today, there are people who use the same names, who serve in the same locations others have served, but they only inhabit the land and the buildings that were conquered and built by those with a "pioneering spirit" in God. Today's inhabitants can tell stories of how things were built and victories were won, but they repeat these stories as someone repeating a historical account.

For those who had the pioneering spirit and trusted God for the facilities, the facilities were never the goal, only a means to the goal.

In some places there are large facilities and large numbers of people to lead, but the pioneers who once used those facilities knew firsthand that God provided them. The pioneers who led those large numbers of people before led a people who knew that their leader had personally trusted God for wisdom and direction because there was no other way to get wisdom and direction.

College students sit in buildings and use facilities that were provided by the faith and sacrifices of others. They will never have an appreciation for those facilities like the people that had to trust God to provide them. For those who had the pioneering spirit and trusted God for the facilities, the facilities were never the goal, only a means to the goal. Their goal was God. They followed God and needed physical facilities to conduct the ministries that God had given them. But the generation following faces the temptation of making the care and maintenance of the buildings the goal, because somehow they cannot understand the faith that was exercised in trusting God for the provision. Growing, pioneering ministries so often degenerate into ministries of maintaining.

Young students sit in the classrooms of Christian schools at desks they had no part in purchasing, in buildings they had no part in building, using facilities they had no part in providing. How can we expect them to have appreciation for what was not firsthand to them?

It is so easy to make a goal out of a by-product, to find something that has been produced as a result of faith in God and make the by-product the goal, and not faith in God the goal.

The pioneer never feels toward the physical facilities the way those who come after the pioneers feel toward the physical facilities. It is the spirit of adventure, following God, the faith life that is most meaningful to the pioneer. We must lift up our eyes and look on the fields. They are white unto harvest. Unless we recapture this pioneering spirit and move from the death of a maintenance ministry, someone will say of us, *"There arose another generation after them, which knew not the LORD, nor yet the works which he had done"* (Judges 2:10).

It is so easy to make a goal out of a by-product, to find something that has been produced as a result of faith in God and make the by-product the goal, and not faith in God the goal.

David said, *"Is there not a cause?"* The mindset of most people in David's day was given to maintaining a good army camp, repairing the tents, continuing to bring in supplies, providing medical care if needed for accidental things that took place around the campsite, watching old soldiers die, talking about how bad things were and how good they used to be, occasionally dreaming of what could be, but never walking down into the valley to face Goliath.

It is because David had a pioneering faith that he realized there was a cause. The cause was not to slay the giant. The Bible plainly states the cause, *"That all the earth may know that there is a God"* (II Samuel 17:46).

There is a fruitful knowledge of Jesus Christ, and there is an unfruitful knowledge of Jesus Christ. The "unfruitful" knowledge is knowing about Jesus Christ. The "fruitful" knowledge is knowing Him. Do you know Him? If you do, it is because you have exercised faith in Him.

May God help us not to run from our obstacles. May God help us to endure the battle. The Lord did not tell Moses that He would kill Pharaoh. He told Moses, "I will go with you to face him." It is in trusting God to help us face our pharaohs that God becomes real to us.

When Elijah stood before King Ahab, he did not say, "I am standing before King Ahab." He said, "I am standing in the presence of God before King Ahab." Trusting God to enable him to deal with Ahab made God real to Elijah.

May the Lord thrust us into the battle, into the thick of the fight. By whatever means necessary, may we find ourselves facing what many believe to be impossible, but those who have a pioneering spirit will know that all things are possible with God.

You may choose to maintain. You may choose to avoid the conflict. You may choose not to launch out into the deep. You may stay in shallow water, or you may choose a road where you expect little resistance; but remember if you do, you will not know God.

Our Lord has commanded us to go into all the world and preach the gospel to every creature. We are to win the lost to Christ and establish

New Testament churches. This work will not be accomplished by means of education and training; it will only be accomplished by people with pioneering spirit, people who believe God for what must be done.

The Bible says in Acts 1:1-8,

> *The former treatise have I made, O Theophilus, of all that Jesus began both to do and teach, until the day in which he was taken up, after that he through the Holy Ghost had given commandments unto the apostles whom he had chosen: to whom also he shewed himself alive after his passion by many infallible proofs, being seen of them forty days, and speaking of the things pertaining to the kingdom of God: and, being assembled together with them, commanded them that they should not depart from Jerusalem, but wait for the promise of the Father, which, saith he, ye have heard of me. For John truly baptized with water; but ye shall be baptized with the Holy Ghost not many days hence. When they therefore were come together, they asked of him, saying, Lord, wilt thou at this time restore again the kingdom to Israel? And he said unto them, It is not for you to know the times or the seasons, which the Father hath put in his own power. But ye shall receive power, after that the Holy Ghost is come upon you: and ye shall be witnesses unto me both in Jerusalem, and in all Judaea, and in Samaria, and unto the uttermost part of the earth.*

Our Lord commanded us to go *"unto the uttermost part of the earth."* Every town, every village, every city, and every community needs a New Testament church. Those of us who know the Lord as our Savior and are part of a Bible-preaching New Testament church should be fully aware that the greatest thing happening in our town is what takes place in and through the local church that is obedient to His command. This is the work of God.

God made us for eternity, not just for time. People get many things they need for time in other places; but they can get what they need for eternity in a New Testament church.

There are certain things we should all understand about the New Testament church. The church started with Christ and His disciples and was empowered at Pentecost. The Lord Jesus gave ordinances to the church. These are the things He ordered that we do—baptism and the Lord's Supper. These are not ministerial ordinances; they are local church ordinances. These things are done under the authority the Lord gave the local New Testament church.

Christ also gave us doctrine, our beliefs and teachings. The sole authority for our faith and practice is the Word of God. We are not creedal people. We do not have creeds that we read and go through repetitiously. We are people of the Book. The Bible, the Word of God, is our sole authority.

Baptists are not Protestants. We are not Catholics. We are not Jews. We love all people, but we are Baptists. When tracing the beginning of our doctrine and principles, we do not find a Martin Luther or a John Calvin or a John Wesley. We find none other than the Lord Jesus Christ. The Lord Jesus gave His disciples a body of doctrine, and because we have an infallible Book that is preserved forever, we can hold the Word of God in our hands and hide it in our hearts. The same body of doctrine the Lord gave His disciples has been handed down through the centuries and delivered to us. It is our solemn responsibility to give it to the next generation.

I am grateful for everyone who is truly a Christian, and I am grateful for the opportunity to tell those who are not saved how to know the Lord Jesus Christ as their Savior. I certainly do not have the idea that the only people who will be in heaven are Baptists. The people who will be in heaven are those who have been washed in the blood of the Lamb and the precious little ones who have died in the safe care and keeping of Christ before they came to the time of accountability. This is in God's hands.

As Christians, we should have a spiritual understanding of the local church. It is the work of churches to start churches. The church I have the privilege of pastoring was started by another church. It is not the work of mission agencies to start churches. It is not the work of Christian colleges to start churches. Starting churches is the work God gave to churches.

The bride of Christ, the church, can give birth. Mission agencies and mission boards can start more mission agencies and mission boards, but it is not their responsibility to start churches. It is the responsibility of churches to start churches.

The simplest definition of a local church is "a group of baptized believers who have voluntarily joined themselves together to carry out the Great Commission." Because it is the responsibility of churches to start churches in the cities, the communities, and the towns where churches are needed, this must be done by other Bible-believing, Bible-preaching churches.

We need to understand the ministry of the local church. Let us give our lives in service to God through the ministry of the local church. God's work in this world is the work of the New Testament church.

The Bible says in Acts 1:8 that we are to be witnesses unto Him *"in Jerusalem, and in all Judaea, and in Samaria, and unto the uttermost part of the earth."*

We must place the emphasis where God places the emphasis, *"unto the uttermost part of the earth."* There is no place to stop. There is no place where we arrive, then end. By the very nature of the New Testament church, it must continue to be a church with a pioneering spirit, always pressing beyond, *"unto the uttermost part of the earth."*

We live in a world of more than six billion people. We live in a country with nearly 300 million people and nearly 3,200 counties. Churches are to plant churches to reach these people with the gospel. What a glorious thing to be a part of a local assembly of baptized believers who hold the Bible as their sole authority for faith and practice! What a privilege to be in a place where children can grow up hearing the Word of God!

We need pioneers. In the New Testament, we find people who pioneered a work for God. By the very fact that the world is against God and we are to go *"into all the world, and preach the gospel to every creature,"* we are going against the grain. It is a pioneering work we must do as we go against the grain of the world and preach the gospel, depending on God to enable us to do the work of winning the lost to Christ and establishing churches.

We can follow the Scriptures and develop a New Testament church pioneer team that can be duplicated into many teams and can be transported anywhere in the world to help people develop a team of pioneers that will go to "a region beyond." That team will train another team of pioneers to go to "a region beyond" and do it again. It is more than activity that we need; we must follow a biblical pattern.

The First Century Church Had a Spiritual Understanding of God's Work in the World

Every one in a New Testament church should have a spiritual understanding of God's work in the world. There is a difference between Israel and the first century church. God is not finished with Israel, but He is working through the church.

The church age had a beginning and the church age will have an ending, as far as the work on earth is concerned. Christ is coming again to receive His bride. From the Bible we learn what the Lord has given His church to do at this time.

The First Century Church Had a Basic Knowledge of Bible Doctrine

Not only should every one of us have an understanding of what God is doing in this world, we should study to attain a basic knowledge of Bible doctrine. I am not afraid of the truth. If you are a biblicist, if you hold to the Scripture and follow correct principles of interpreting Scripture, you will know the truth because the Holy Spirit will teach you the truth. All of us need a basic knowledge of Bible doctrine. From that we can continue to learn more and more of the Lord and His work.

The First Century Church Had a Heart for World Evangelism

All of us need a heart for world evangelism. There should not be one little group in the church that has a heart for world evangelism while everyone else watches the work being done.

We should study world geography as it applies to world evangelism. For example, if we hear something about Spain, we should be thinking, "Are they getting the gospel in Spain? Where are the New Testament churches in Spain? What cities are these churches in? Where are unevangelized areas?" This kind of thing should be on the hearts of Christian people because we are God's children and God has given us His work to do in this world. His work is bringing the lost to Christ and establishing New Testament churches.

Let me introduce you to some New Testament church pioneers. Let us observe these individuals from Scripture and recognize what is particular to their lives. Pray that God will use you in some way as a New Testament church pioneer, bringing the lost to Christ and starting a New Testament church.

It may be a journey you make that takes a few weeks. It may take a few months. It may be a place where you go and spend the rest of your life.

Our Lord will be pleased when churches are actually functioning and doing what He gave us to do. A New Testament church will find that it is unnatural not to be planting churches. It is perfectly natural for a church, functioning the way God wants it to function, to be giving birth to church after church and teaching those churches from God's Word that it is their responsibility to birth other churches.

Remember that church planting is not the goal. It is a by-product of obedience to the Lord Jesus Christ.

Remember that church planting is not the goal. It is a by-product of obedience to the Lord Jesus Christ. I recommend you read many of the helpful things written by A. B. Simpson. The Lord used him to do a mighty work. My ideas concerning this pioneering ministry were greatly influenced by his writings.

For those who are not preachers or evangelists or do not consider themselves to be missionaries, God wants to use them in a dynamic way to start New Testament churches.

Chapter Eleven

The Apostle Paul
Providing Christian Literature

Let us begin with the apostle Paul. In II Timothy chapter four, we come to the end of Paul's life where he said in verses six and seven, *"For I am now ready to be offered, and the time of my departure is at hand. I have fought a good fight, I have finished my course, I have kept the faith."*

He said in I Corinthians 2:2, *"For I determined not to know any thing among you, save Jesus Christ, and him crucified."* He abandoned himself to God to be God's missionary pioneer. God used him as a human penman for so much of the New Testament.

Allow Paul to represent to us, not only the pioneering spirit, but what people need in print to help them understand God's Word and the things of God. Scripture is complete; we will not get any more of it. I am thinking of the printing of Bibles and Christian literature.

One of the things we must have if we are going to start churches is printed material to put into the hands of families, children, and young people. No doubt, we should be able to get off a plane or out of a car anywhere in the world with nothing but the Word of God in our hands and be able to instruct people in what the Lord wants them to do. But all of us realize that gospel tracts, gospel literature, and the material we teach in our Bible-teaching Sunday School are all a vital part of helping us as we look to God and God's Word. Let us associate Paul with printed materials and those who have a pioneering spirit to get Bibles and Christ-centered literature into the hands of others.

Philip
Following the Lord's Leading

We actually need many Philips. The Bible tells us a number of things about Philip, this deacon, missionary, and evangelist.

In Acts chapter eight, there had been a great revival. Philip had been right in the middle of it. The Bible says in verses twenty-six through thirty-one,

> *And the angel of the Lord spake unto Philip, saying, Arise, and go toward the south unto the way that goeth down from Jerusalem unto Gaza, which is desert. And he arose and went: and, behold, a man of Ethiopia, an eunuch of great authority under Candace queen of the Ethiopians, who had the charge of all her treasure, and had come to Jerusalem for to worship, was returning, and sitting in his chariot read Esaias the prophet. Then the Spirit said unto Philip, Go near, and join thyself to this chariot. And Philip ran thither to him, and heard him read the prophet Esaias, and said, Understandest thou what thou readest? And he said, How can I, except some man should guide me? And he desired Philip that he would come up and sit with him.*

Observe the story of the Ethiopian eunuch and how Philip led him to the Lord, reading to him the fifty-third chapter of Isaiah, pointing him to Christ. The point I wish to make with Philip is that he was a man who allowed God to lead him to the place of the Lord's choosing. No one, using his own wisdom or his own understanding, would have left a city of great revival and gone to one Ethiopian eunuch in the desert. Churches and areas of God's great blessing and influence are the very places from which people must go out to other areas of need. Our God leads His children.

Do you imagine the place of greatest need to be the place of greatest population without churches? The place of greatest need is the place of God's leading. Many people need to understand that we must seek God's face because there are out-of-the-way places, there are villages, towns, and cities all across America and around the world that God will direct us to as we pray and seek His face. Begin to pray for the small towns across America without a church.

Barnabas
Contributing to Special Needs

In Acts 4:36-37 the Bible says, *"And Joses, who by the apostles was surnamed Barnabas, (which is, being interpreted, The son of consolation,) a Levite, and of the country of Cyprus, having land, sold it, and brought the money, and laid it at the apostles' feet."* Barnabas was a layman, a businessman. He was a man of means. He sold a piece of land he had and gave the money to the work of God.

One of the tremendous needs in the work of God is the work of laymen and businessmen realizing that God wants to use them to plant churches. There are laymen and businessmen who could make contributions financially to God's work because God has blessed them in a unique way.

There are also laymen and businessmen like Barnabas who can help start a church. They can reach other laymen and businessmen and teach them that they can serve in a New Testament church and help that church to start other churches.

Epaphras
Praying Fervently

The Bible says in Colossians 4:12, *"Epaphras, who is one of you, a servant of Christ, saluteth you, always labouring fervently for you in prayers, that ye may stand perfect and complete in all the will of God."*

There are many ways God can speak to us about praying. Here we find a profound statement, *"labouring fervently for you in prayers."*

No New Testament church pioneer could do a greater work than prayer. Epaphras gave himself to prayer.

Remember that all the members of this team will have singular responsibilities but will all work together. They are people who have a spiritual understanding of God's Word, have a basic knowledge of Bible doctrine, and have a heart for world evangelism.

Luke
Providing Unique Skills

In Colossians 4:14 the Bible says, *"Luke, the beloved physician..."* Luke represents people with special skills. We have medical doctors in our church. We have many other people who have special skills. They are not preachers; they are not evangelists; they are not missionaries; they are Christians who love God and have special skills. They can be New Testament pioneers.

We have people who can build and people who can design. There are people who are architects. There are people who are engineers who have special skills. They must also be soul winners and go. We need New Testament church pioneers on this team who are like Luke, people who love God and have special skills.

The apostle Paul talked about only Luke being with him, standing by his side encouraging him. God has blessed many people in churches with special skills that could be used on a New Testament church pioneering team to start other churches.

Aquila and Priscilla
Encouraging New Converts

In Acts 18 we find a couple, Aquila and Priscilla, tenderly working for the Lord. These are people who are given to the ministry of encouragement. In verses twenty-four through twenty-six, the Bible says,

> *And a certain Jew named Apollos, born at Alexandria, an eloquent man, and mighty in the*

> *scriptures, came to Ephesus. This man was instructed in the way of the Lord; and being fervent in the spirit, he spake and taught diligently the things of the Lord, knowing only the baptism of John. And he began to speak boldly in the synagogue: whom when Aquila and Priscilla had heard, they took him unto them, and expounded unto him the way of God more perfectly.*

This couple was greatly used of God. Of course, there are other references to them in the New Testament. The mighty preacher Apollos is thought by some to have been more eloquent than any other preacher in the New Testament. Here was a mighty man of God. Apollos needed someone with more maturity and understanding to take him aside and teach him the way of God more perfectly. This couple, Aquila and Priscilla, did just that.

Often I see husbands and wives taking a young preacher under their wing, nurturing him, helping him, and encouraging him. There are many Aquilas and Priscillas who could be mightily used of God to help people grow in the grace and knowledge of the Lord and know the way of God more perfectly.

TIMOTHY
Developing Disciples

The Bible says in II Timothy 2:1-2, *"Thou therefore, my son, be strong in the grace that is in Christ Jesus. And the things that thou hast heard of me among many witnesses, the same commit thou to faithful men, who shall be able to teach others also."* Timothy represents for us the area of discipleship.

Paul called Timothy his son in the ministry. He wrote to him and said in II Timothy 3:15, *"And that from a child thou hast known the holy scriptures, which are able to make thee wise unto salvation through faith which is in Christ Jesus."* Timothy had been brought along in the Word of God.

The apostle, under the inspiration of the Spirit of God, gave Timothy this principle in II Timothy 2:2, *"And the things that thou hast heard of me among many witnesses, the same commit thou to faithful men, who shall be able to teach others also."*

May the Lord give us a pioneering spirit like these first century Christians had. May we press on to the uttermost part of the earth in the power of His Holy Spirit.

XII

Personal Accountability to God in the First Century Church

The Bible, the Word of God, is the sole authority for our faith and practice. If the Bible speaks about something, then we should speak about it. If the Bible is silent on a subject, then we are to be silent on that subject. We are people of the Book. We make no apology for this. What we believe and teach comes from the Word of God. Let us place the emphasis where God places the emphasis.

When we say that the Bible is our sole authority, we are speaking of all the Scriptures, the whole and its parts. We should preach the whole counsel of God. In the Bible we find the gospel–the death, burial, and resurrection of Jesus Christ. We should proclaim the gospel because Jesus Christ said that we are to take the gospel message to every creature. When we open the sixty-six books of the Bible, we find more than the gospel. Of course, that scarlet thread of redemption runs throughout all the Bible, but the whole counsel of God must be proclaimed.

Chapter Twelve

If we are going to be spiritual people, we must be scriptural people. It is impossible to be a spiritual person without being a scriptural person.

The Bible says in Romans 14:11-12, *"For it is written, As I live, saith the Lord, every knee shall bow to me, and every tongue shall confess to God. So then every one of us shall give account of himself to God."*

"Every one of us shall give account of himself to God." We are personally accountable to God.

In our nation we hear people talk about religious tolerance. Religious tolerance is something created by government. It is a "gift" from government. Religious tolerance is something man has made. Soul liberty is something God established when He created us. We find the clear teaching of this in His Word. Soul liberty is a gift from God! God's Word says in Galatians 5:1, *"Stand fast therefore in the liberty wherewith Christ hath made us free, and be not entangled again with the yoke of bondage."*

The liberty of our souls does not rest upon the legal documents of our nation–this liberty is rooted in the Word of God. This individual freedom of the soul is inherent in man's nature as God created him. Man is responsible for his choices, but he is free to choose.

This powerful declaration about this position taken historically by Baptist people was made by J. D. Freeman in 1905:

> Our demand has been not simply for religious toleration, but religious liberty; not sufferance merely, but freedom; and that not for ourselves alone, but for all men. We did not stumble upon the doctrine. It inheres in the very essence of our belief. Christ is Lord of all....The conscience is the servant only of God, and is not subject to the will of man. This truth has indestructible life. Crucify it and the third day it

> will rise again. Bury it in the sepulcher and the stone will be rolled away, while the keepers become as dead men....Steadfastly refusing to bend our necks under the yoke of bondage, we have scrupulously withheld our hands from imposing that yoke upon others.... Of martyr blood our hands are clean. We have never invoked the sword of temporal power to aid the sword of the Spirit. We have never passed an ordinance inflicting a civic disability on any man because of his religious views, be he Protestant or Papist, Jew, or Turk, or infidel. In this regard there is no blot on our escutcheon [family coat of arms].

Remember, when we are talking about individual soul liberty and the relationship of the church and the state, in America our Constitution does not place the church over the state or the state over the church. Most importantly, Scripture places them side by side, each operating independently of the other. This means there is freedom in the church and freedom in the state. Each is sovereign within the sphere of the authority God has given to each of them (Matthew 22:21).

Read carefully this statement made by Charles Spurgeon concerning Baptist people:

> We believe that the Baptists are the original Christians. We did not commence our existence at the Reformation; we were reformers before Luther or Calvin were born. We never came from the Church of Rome, for we were never in it, but we have an unbroken line up to the apostles themselves. We have always existed from the very days of Christ, and our principles, sometimes veiled and forgotten, like a river which may travel underground for a little season, have always had honest and holy adherents.

> Persecuted alike by Romanists and Protestants of almost every sect, yet there has never existed a government holding Baptist principles which persecuted others; nor, I believe, any body of Baptists ever held it to be right to put the consciences of others under the control of man. We have ever been ready to suffer, as our martyrologies will prove, but we are not ready to accept any help from the State, to prostitute the purity of the Bride of Christ to any alliance with government, and we will never make the church, although the Queen, the despot over the consciences of men.

Spurgeon, a Baptist by conviction, affirmed that we never held it to be right "to put the consciences of others under the control of men." I am rather troubled when I see so many people who claim to be Baptists who do not understand why they are Baptists. We should be able to defend our position and do it biblically. If we are people who know and love the Lord and His Word and if the Bible is our sole authority for faith and practice, then we have no reason to be ashamed of the position we take. May God not only help us to take this position, but to take it with holy boldness and compassion. May He help us to be able to take His Word in hand and heart and defend what we believe to a lost and dying world.

Man is responsible for his choices, but he is free to choose.

So much of what we have to enjoy in our country can be credited to Baptist people. For example, when studying the history of our nation, you are going to find that the Virginia Baptists were almost solely responsible for the First Amendment being added to our Constitution. We enjoy this freedom to worship God as our conscience dictates because of the influence of Baptist people on the founding fathers of our nation.

We do not believe it is right to exercise any control or coercion of any kind over the souls of men. Where did this conviction come from? We find it in the Bible, but someone imparted it to the founding fathers. It became the law of the land, and it should remain the law of the land. We need to understand it. It comes out of the clear teaching of God's Word concerning the subject of soul liberty.

THE FIRST CENTURY CHURCH TAUGHT PERSONAL ACCOUNTABILITY TO GOD

We find this accountability in the opening verses of God's Word. When God created man, He created man capable of giving a personal account of himself to God. God did not create puppets; He created people. He gave man the right to choose. That is why we find the man Adam choosing to sin and to disobey God in Genesis chapter three. Of his own volition he chose to sin and disobey God. Genesis 1:27 says, *"So God created man in his own image, in the image of God created he him; male and female created he them."* We were made in God's image, and when God made us in His image, He made us with the ability to choose. Eve was deceived and disobeyed God, but Adam chose to die rather than to live without Eve. He willingly chose to disobey the Lord.

If we are going to be spiritual people, we must be scriptural people.

It is not right to try to force one's religion or belief upon another individual. He has a God-given right to believe anything he wishes to believe. This does not mean, however, that he can be a Christian by believing anything he wishes to believe, because Jesus Christ said that there is only one way to heaven. He said in John 14:6, *"I am the way, the truth, and the life: no man cometh unto the Father, but by me."* He is the only way to God. The only way of salvation is the Lord Jesus Christ.

> *When God created man, He created man capable of giving a personal account of himself to God.*

In this age of tolerance, people say that nothing is really wrong. The same people who say that no belief is wrong will not accept the truth that one belief can be the only way that is right. The truth is, you may believe anything you choose, but God has declared that there is only one way to Him and that is through His Son, Jesus Christ. He is the only way of salvation–that is why He suffered and died for our sins. The only way to know God is through His Son, the Lord Jesus Christ.

Someone is certain to ask, "Who are you to declare that everyone else's religion is wrong?" We are saying that everyone has a right to choose his own way, but God has clearly taught us in His Word that there is only one way to Him. The Lord Jesus says in John 10:9, *"I am the door: by me if any man enter in, he shall be saved, and shall go in and out, and find pasture."* The first century church was taught this by the Lord Jesus Christ.

No human being is going to live on this earth without being sinned against by others. Many children are sinned against greatly by their own parents. However, we cannot go through life blaming others for the person we are, because God has made us in such a way that we have an individual accountability to God. This comes out of our soul liberty and our right to choose and respond to things in a way that God would have us respond to them. God has made us in His image.

Again, He did not make us puppets or robots; He made us people, created in His image with the ability to choose our own way.

Romans 14:11-12 says, *"For it is written, As I live, saith the Lord, every knee shall bow to me, and every tongue shall confess to God. So then every one of us shall give account of himself to God."* We are responsible because we have direct access to God. God has given us His Word, the Holy Spirit, and access to the throne by prayer. We, therefore, must answer personally to God at the judgment seat because God communicates to us directly.

People do not like to be held personally accountable for their actions. The truth of the Word of God is that every individual is personally accountable to God. You are personally accountable to God. In other words, you are going to meet God in judgment some day. I am going to meet God in judgment some day. All of us are going to stand before the Lord some day and answer to Him. We are individually accountable to God. Since the state cannot answer for us to God, it has no right to dictate our consciences.

We are individually accountable to God. Since the state cannot answer for us to God, it has no right to dictate our consciences.

We live in a country where there are many false religions. As Bible-believing people, we would defend the right of anyone in our land to worship as he sees fit to worship. This is unheard of in most of the world. If a man is a Moslem, I do not agree with his Islamic religion, but I defend his right to worship as he sees fit to worship. The clear teaching of the Catholic church teaches that salvation comes through Mary, but this is not the teaching of the Bible. We must take a stand against false religions, but we must also defend the right of people to worship as they choose to worship. Why? Because individual soul liberty is a gift from God to every human being.

Chapter Twelve

If we truly believe that the Bible teaches individual soul liberty and personal accountability to God, then it is a truth that will endure to all generations.

John Bunyan is the man who gave us *Pilgrim's Progress*. This wonderful book was planned during Bunyan's prison experience and written when he was released. The trial of John Bunyan took place on October 3, 1660. John Bunyan spent twelve years in jail for his convictions about individual soul liberty, failure to attend the Church of England, and for preaching the Word of God. During his trial, John stood before the judge who was interested in hearing John Bunyan state his case. The judge said, "In that case, then, this court would be profoundly interested in your response to them."

Part of John Bunyan's response follows:

> Thank you, M'lord. And may I say that I am grateful for the opportunity to respond. Firstly, the depositions speak the truth. I have never attended services in the Church of England, nor do I intend ever to do so. Secondly, it is no secret that I preach the Word of God whenever, wherever, and to whomever He pleases to grant me opportunity to do so.
>
> Having said that, M'lord, there is a weightier issue that I am constrained to address. I have no choice but to acknowledge my awareness of the law which I am accused of transgressing. Likewise, I have no choice but to confess my guilt in my transgression of it. As true as these things are, I must affirm that I neither regret breaking the law, nor repent of having broken it. Further, I must warn you that I have no intention in future of conforming to it. It is, on its face, an unjust law, a law against which honorable men cannot shrink from protesting. In truth, M'lord, it violates an infinitely higher law–the right of every

man to seek God in his own way, unhindered by any temporal power. That, M'lord, is my response.

Remember that Bunyan was responding as to why he would not do all that he was doing for God within the confines of the Church of England. The transcription goes on to say:

> Judge: This court would remind you, sir, that we are not here to debate the merits of the law. We are here to determine if you are, in fact, guilty of violating it.
>
> Bunyan: Perhaps, M'lord, that is why you are here, but it is most certainly not why I am here. I am here because you compel me to be here. All I ask is to be left alone to preach and to teach as God directs me. As, however, I must be here, I cannot fail to use these circumstances to speak against what I know to be an unjust and odious edict.
>
> Judge: Let me understand you. You are arguing that every man has a right, given him by Almighty God, to seek the Deity in his own way, even if he chooses without the benefit of the English Church?
>
> Bunyan: That is precisely what I am arguing, M'lord. Or without benefit of any church.
>
> Judge: Do you know what you are saying? What of Papists and Quakers? What of pagan Mohammedans? Have these the right to seek God in their own misguided way?
>
> Bunyan: Even these, M'lord.

Judge: May I ask if you are particularly sympathetic to the views of these or other such deviant religious societies?

Bunyan: I am not, M'lord.

Judge: Yet, you affirm a God-given right to hold any alien religious doctrine that appeals to the warped minds of men?

Bunyan: I do, M'lord.

Judge: I find your views impossible of belief. And what of those who, if left to their own devices, would have no interest in things heavenly? Have they the right to be allowed to continue unmolested in their error?

Bunyan: It is my fervent belief that they do, M'lord.

Judge: And on what basis, might I ask, can you make such rash affirmations?

Bunyan: On the basis, M'lord, that a man's religious views–or lack of them–are matters between his conscience and his God, and are not the business of the Crown, the Parliament, or even, with all due respect, M'lord, of this court. However much I may be in disagreement with another man's sincerely held religious beliefs, neither I nor any other may disallow his right to hold those beliefs. No man's rights in these affairs are secure if every other man's rights are not equally secure.

I do not know of anyone who could have expressed the whole idea of soul liberty and personal accountability in the words of man any more clearly than Bunyan stated in 1660. Every man can seek God as he pleases. This means that we cannot force our religious faith or teaching on anyone. It means clearly that no one can be coerced into being a Baptist and believing what we believe. It means that we can do no arm-twisting, or anything of that sort, to make anyone believe what we believe. Every man has been created by God with the ability to choose to follow God or to follow some other god.

Personal accountability to God is a distinctive of our faith. It is something we believe, and out of this distinctive comes other biblical distinctives that we identify with as Baptist people.

The First Century Church Taught the Priesthood of Every Believer

The priesthood of the believer means that every believer can go to God through the merit of Jesus Christ. Christ and Christ alone is the only way to God. All of us who have trusted Christ as Savior enjoy the glorious privilege of the priesthood of the believer and can access God through the merits of our Lord and Savior Jesus Christ.

The Bible says in I Timothy 2:1-6,

> *I exhort therefore, that, first of all, supplications, prayers, intercessions, and giving of thanks, be made for all men; for kings, and for all that are in authority; that we may lead a quiet and peaceable life in all godliness and honesty. For this is good and acceptable in the sight of God our Saviour; who will have all men to be saved, and to come unto the*

> *knowledge of the truth. For there is one God, and one mediator between God and men, the man Christ Jesus; who gave himself a ransom for all, to be testified in due time.*

Take special note of verse five, *"For there is one God, and one mediator between God and men, the man Christ Jesus."* Any man, anywhere in this world can go to God through the Lord Jesus Christ.

> *We are responsible because we have direct access to God. God has given us His Word, the Holy Spirit, and access to the throne by prayer.*

I Peter 2:9 says, *"But ye are a chosen generation, a royal priesthood, an holy nation, a peculiar people; that ye should shew forth the praises of him who hath called you out of darkness into his marvellous light."*

You have access to God. You can personally talk to God. You can take your needs to the Lord. Whatever your needs are, you can take those needs to the Lord. You, as an individual Christian, can go to God through the Lord Jesus Christ, your High Priest who *"ever liveth to make intercession"* for you (Hebrews 7:25).

We have no merit of our own. We do not accumulate merit. People may make reference to a time of meritorious service someone has rendered, but we cannot build up "good works" that get us through to God. Each day, we must come before God as needy sinners approaching Him through the finished work of Christ and Christ alone.

The Bible teaches the personal accountability of every human being to God. We cannot force our religion on anyone or make anyone a believer. We cannot force someone to be a Christian. Think of how wrong it is to take babies and allow them later in life to think they have become Christians by an act of infant baptism. Yes, people have a right to practice infant baptism, but we do not believe this is biblical because faith cannot be forced or coerced.

If I have discovered the truth in Christ and believe that God's Word is inerrant, infallible, and eternal, certainly I want my own children to believe that. I have no greater joy than that they walk in truth, but I cannot make my sons Christians. They must choose Christ of their own will.

We will never make a difference without being willing to be different. It is Christ who makes us different.

I have six beautiful grandchildren. There is a real heaven and a real hell. The Bible clearly teaches this. The only way to heaven and the only way to miss hell is by trusting Christ and Christ alone as Savior. However, I cannot make those grandchildren Christians no matter how much I desire to. They must individually trust Christ as their Savior.

There are places in the world where the state is under a religion. There are places in the world where religion is under the state–the state controls the fate of people. This is not taught in the Bible. Then, there are countries like ours where the church and the state operate side by side.

The First Century Church Recognized the Power of Influence

Where does this teaching of the priesthood of every believer and our personal accountability to God lead us? It leads us to recognize the importance of the power of influence. This is the tool God has given us.

I want to give you an Old Testament example to explain the place of the New Testament church. There is a difference between Israel and the church; I am not trying to place the church in the Old Testament, but let us use this as an illustration. Remember, God has always had a people.

Judges 21:25 tells us, *"In those days there was no king in Israel: every man did that which was right in his own eyes."* This was a land of anarchy. Every man did what was right in his own eyes. In the days of the judges, every man wanted to do what he thought was right with no fixed point of reference.

> *The world does not need another imitation of itself.*

God's Word continues to describe this time of judges in Ruth 1:1, *"Now it came to pass in the days when the judges ruled, that there was a famine in the land."* God begins to tell us about a man named Elimelech, his wife Naomi, and his sons. He brings us to the beautiful love story of Ruth and Boaz. God tells us that at the same time in which the judges ruled, when there was anarchy in the land, this beautiful love story of Boaz and Ruth took place.

This story gives us interesting insight as to the responsibility of believers living in the midst of unbelief. In the midst of everything that is happening, we are to share the beautiful love story of the Lord Jesus Christ and His bride. We need to tell people about the Savior.

The same truth is found throughout the Word of God. Philippians 2:15 states, *"That ye may be blameless and harmless, the sons of God, without rebuke, in the midst of a crooked and perverse nation, among whom ye shine as lights in the world."*

We are *"in the midst of a crooked and perverse nation."* This is why the Lord Jesus said in Matthew 5:16, *"Let your light so shine before men, that they may see your good works, and glorify your Father which is in heaven."* Let your light shine!

The more a church becomes like the world, the less influence it is going to have in the world. Preaching ceases, and churches only have dialogue. Singing that is sacred is taken out, and the world's music comes in. What so many are attempting to do in order to build up their ministry is actually what will cause the demise of their ministry. We will never make a difference without being willing to be different. It is Christ who makes us different. A sick church cannot help a sick world. The worldly church is a great harm to the world. Please remember that the world does not need another imitation of itself.

We cannot force people to become Christians or force our religion on people. It is not right to violate another man's will; he must choose of his own volition to trust Christ or reject Christ. When we understand this, then we understand the powerful tool of influence. We must live godly lives and be what God wants us to be. We must be lights in a dark world as we live in the midst of a crooked generation. The only tool we have to use is influence, not force. As we separate ourselves to God and live godly lives, only then do we have a testimony.

Separation to God and from the world is not the enemy of evangelism; it is the essential of evangelism. There can be no evangelism without separation to God from the world because we have no other tool to use. We cannot make people believe what we believe to be the truth. They must choose of their own will. We must so identify with the Lord Jesus in His beauty, glory, and holiness, that He will be lifted up, and people will come to Him.

Chapter Twelve

As this world becomes increasingly worse, we will appear more off-the-wall and ridiculous to an unbelieving world. The temptation will come again and again for us to simply cave in.

Because of what we find in the Bible about soul liberty, personal accountability, and the priesthood of every believer, we must use the power of influence to win the lost to Christ. If we conform to the world, we lose our influence.

The first century church was taught this by the Lord Jesus, and they demonstrated to an unbelieving world the reality of knowing God by the changed lives they lived. May the Lord help us to be unashamed to bear His reproach and be identified with our Lord Jesus Christ.

XIII

The Faith of the First Century Church

he Lord Jesus loved the church and gave Himself for it. Often we speak incorrectly of the church, as if there is some "national" church, when we say "the church in America." Even our founding fathers in America recognized the danger of a national church. We should speak correctly by referring to "churches," individual churches, local New Testament churches.

Throughout the New Testament we find that the first century church moved forward by faith. The Bible says in II Corinthians 8:1-7,

> *Moreover, brethren, we do you to wit of the grace of God bestowed on the churches of Macedonia; how that in a great trial of affliction the abundance of their joy and their deep poverty abounded unto the riches of their liberality. For to their power, I bear record, yea, and beyond their power they were willing of themselves; praying us with much entreaty that we*

> *would receive the gift, and take upon us the fellowship of the ministering to the saints. And this they did, not as we hoped, but first gave their own selves to the Lord, and unto us by the will of God. Insomuch that we desired Titus, that as he had begun, so he would also finish in you the same grace also. Therefore, as ye abound in every thing, in faith, and utterance, and knowledge, and in all diligence, and in your love to us, see that ye abound in this grace also.*

Make note of two words in verse seven, *"in faith."* Remember that the apostle Paul is writing to churches.

The Bible says in I Thessalonians 1:3, *"Remembering without ceasing your work of faith, and labour of love, and patience of hope in our Lord Jesus Christ, in the sight of God and our Father."* Notice the word *"faith"* in verse three.

In chapter three of this same book, the sixth verse says, *"But now when Timotheus came from you unto us, and brought us good tidings of your faith and charity, and that ye have good remembrance of us always, desiring greatly to see us, as we also to see you."* Note the words *"your faith"* in this verse. Then the Bible says in verse seven, *"Therefore, brethren, we were comforted over you in all our affliction and distress by your faith."* Make note again of the expression, *"your faith."*

Then in II Thessalonians 1:3 the Word of God says, *"We are bound to thank God always for you, brethren, as it is meet, because that your faith groweth exceedingly, and the charity of every one of you all toward each other aboundeth."* We see again the expression, *"your faith."*

Notice verse eleven says, *"Wherefore also we pray always for you, that our God would count you worthy of this calling, and fulfil all the good pleasure of his goodness, and the work of faith with power."* Notice the word *"faith"* given to us once again.

The Bible says in Romans 1:8, *"First, I thank my God through Jesus Christ for you all, that your faith is spoken of throughout the whole world."* Make note of the expression, *"your faith."*

The faith of the first century church provides a pattern for us today. Just because there is a building somewhere at a certain street address, with the name "church" written on it, does not mean that a church meeting actually takes place there. The people who come inside that building may refer to themselves as a church, but do they have faith in God? The New Testament church moves forward by faith. The believing church, the church with faith in God, brings to their ministry what God can accomplish in them and through them.

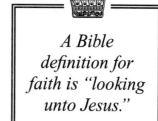

A Bible definition for faith is "looking unto Jesus."

Let us have more; let us do more; let us be more than what men can have and do and be. If all we can get is what we can muster up, we are not going to get much. We certainly are not going to get what we need. We must be people of faith in God.

It is important to understand that the Bible says in Hebrews 11:1, *"Now faith is the substance of things hoped for, the evidence of things not seen."* This is faith described. Faith is defined in Hebrews 12:2 where the Bible says, *"Looking unto Jesus the author and finisher of our faith."* A Bible definition for faith is *"looking unto Jesus."*

Every time I come to this expression, I cannot help but think of what I have read concerning Hudson Taylor, the missionary to China. He said that at one point in his ministry, he was too weak to pray, too weak to write, too weak to preach, too weak to teach. He simply collapsed in the arms of the Lord Jesus and looked to Him to sustain him and strengthen him.

Chapter Thirteen

"Looking unto Jesus the author and finisher of our faith." There is no cap, no ceiling that man knows to be placed on a church that will look unto Jesus Christ. Our God wants to do a mighty work in this world; there is no doubt about that. The Bible says He can do exceeding abundantly above all we ask or think (Ephesians 3:20). In other words, no one has ever dreamed of doing anything as great as what God can do.

Often we talk about people with vision. Understand that real vision in the biblical sense can only come from God. Vision means revelation, or what God reveals to a man. We get our vision from God. God gives us vision and this vision enables us to see the world as God sees it, and we want in this world what God wants in this world. We want accomplished in our lives and the lives of others what God wants accomplished.

God gives us vision. In reality, I cannot give you vision. I cannot "cast" the vision to others. I can talk about things that God has led me to do, things that I believe God wants all of us collectively to do; but if you are going to get vision, it must come from God.

In other words, as a believer, the same Holy Spirit that indwells you indwells me. We are talking about God the Holy Spirit living in us–coequal, coexistent, eternally existent with God the Father and God the Son. God the Holy Spirit lives in us. We communicate with God by His Spirit. He speaks with us. He deals with us through His Word. He deals with us through circumstances. He deals with us through other Christians.

God gives us vision. So if I say to you, "I want you to pray about something, seek the face of God, and find out what God wants you to do," it is altogether possible for you to do just that. You are to seek the face of God and find out what God wants you to do.

So often in my own life I am dealing with things that are too difficult for me, things that frustrate me. Sometimes this is obvious to other people. My temptation is to try to stand toe to toe and deal with those things, but there is such a thing as turning away from that and turning to the Lord and asking God as we look unto Him, "Lord, help me."

It does not take long for us to reach the end of ourselves. We go until we run out of steam, out of strength; but there is a fountain that never runs dry. There is a river that flows within us. There is a place to go that always satisfies, and that place is the Person of Jesus Christ. Look to Him!

God is only real to us as we faith Him. He has made it this way. The Christian life cannot be lived by sight. It must be lived by faith.

I want to try to explain a few things to you because I believe we are guilty of some of these things and we need to understand them. Prayer cannot be substituted for faith.

There are so many of us who go through the motions of prayer. Dr. John R. Rice, a dear servant of God who is now in heaven, wrote a wonderful book on prayer. It is acclaimed by many people as the greatest book ever written on prayer. Of course, the greatest book ever written on prayer is the Bible, but I know what they mean by their comments concerning Dr. Rice's book. Dr. Rice tried to simplify the thing for people by saying that prayer is asking and the answer to prayer is receiving. He tried to keep it so simple. Prayer is asking and answer to prayer is receiving.

The Bible says in James 1:1-4,

> *James, a servant of God and of the Lord Jesus Christ, to the twelve tribes which are scattered abroad, greeting. My brethren, count it all joy when ye fall into divers temptations; knowing this, that the trying of your faith worketh patience. But let patience have her perfect work, that ye may be perfect and entire, wanting nothing.*

Chapter Thirteen

I love the language of the Bible. Men talk about being "focused," but God speaks of *"looking unto Jesus."* Men talk about being "balanced," but God speaks of being complete in Christ. Nothing should be substituted in the Christian's life for the language of Scripture. It is convicting. It is powerful. It is penetrating. It has authority.

> *There is a river that flows within us. There is a place to go that always satisfies, and that place is the Person of Jesus Christ. Look to Him!*

Is it more authoritative to say, "Get your life in focus" or to say "Look unto Jesus"? What does it mean to get your life in focus? Is it more authoritative to say, "We want to be balanced" or to say, "Let's be complete in Christ"? There is nothing like the language of Scripture.

In James 1:5 the Bible says, *"If any of you lack wisdom, let him ask of God, that giveth to all men liberally, and upbraideth not; and it shall be given him."* God says to ask. He will not scold you for it. Verse six says, *"But let him ask in faith, nothing wavering. For he that wavereth is like a wave of the sea driven with the wind and tossed."*

Many times as a church we pray, and we think because we have gone through the motions of prayer that we have faith in God. This type of prayer cannot be substituted for faith. We must keep this clear in our minds. We want to be a church of faith in God.

When the apostle Paul wrote to the church in Rome, he talked about their faith being spoken of. In the margin of my Bible, I have written a number of things that I want to be characteristic of the testimony of the church I pastor.

We Believe God's Word

The first thing concerning the testimony of our church should be that we believe God's Word. Our sole authority for faith and practice is the Word of God. Never be ashamed to ask, "What does the Bible say?" Stand firmly on the Word of God.

We Believe the Church Was Established by the Lord Jesus Christ

We should have the conviction that the church was established by the Lord Jesus Christ. He is our only head.

We Believe Christ Satisfies

People should also know that we believe Christ satisfies. He is enough. He is sufficient. Our sufficiency is in Him. He does not have the answer; He is the answer. When you have Him, you have everything else you need.

We Believe God Hears and Answers Prayer

We believe that God hears and answers prayer. Let this be the testimony of our church! We know that God hears and answers prayer.

We Attempt Great Things for God

By faith we attempt great things for God. I use this so that you might understand, but the word *great* is a word that is overused. In the end, God will decide who is great and what is great; but what I mean by this is that we should live beyond the limitations placed on us by men and what they believe can be done. We must live beyond man-made goals and objectives.

We Faithfully Attend the Services of the Church

Let it be said that we faithfully attend the services of the church, *"Not forsaking the assembling of ourselves together, as the manner of some is"* (Hebrews 10:25). We should understand why we meet together and seek to please the Lord in our meetings.

We Believe the Christian Life Is a Holy Life

Our God is holy and He has commanded us to be holy. We should be holy men and holy women. These are expressions we find in the Bible. The Christian life is a holy life.

In this generation, many who claim to be Christians live lives of impurity and unholiness. This does not line up with the Bible. We should be holy people.

We Keep the Sacred Covenant of Marriage

I grew up in a broken home. My mother suffered extreme physical abuse. It was dangerous for her to live with my father. Their marriage ended in divorce.

We should have compassion for anyone who is hurt this way. If our convictions run high, may they never run any higher than our compassion runs deep.

In a church like ours, of course people should stay together. They should understand that it is the testimony of our church to keep their marriage together. That marriage represents the wonderful union between Christ and His bride.

I understand that things happen and people go through horrible failures. My heart goes out to them. But let our testimony be that we make much of the covenant of marriage.

We Give a Clear Presentation of the Gospel

We are not ashamed of the gospel of Christ. We give a clear presentation of the gospel of Christ. We understand the gospel and we teach and preach the gospel.

Our Worship Services Bring Honor and Glory to the Lord Jesus Christ

We are not a contemporary church. The pulpit is for preaching, not a bulletin board for religious activity. Remember, our faith is a treasured heritage and not a contemporary experiment.

We Live Changed Lives

"Therefore if any man be in Christ, he is a new creature" (II Corinthians 5:17). It is the responsibility of every child of God to demonstrate the reality of knowing Christ by the life he lives.

We Live in Submission to the Headship of Jesus Christ

I mean by this that we do not bow to denominationalism. Each New Testament church is an independent congregation, and we answer to our heavenly headquarters. The Lord Jesus Christ is our only head. Never allow denominationalism to take the place of Christ.

We Have Holy Spirit Power and We Labor in the Strength of the Lord

We need God's power to do God's work. Be filled with the Holy Spirit. This is His command.

Our Families Read the Bible and Pray Together

Let our church be a church with the testimony that families read the Bible and pray together. This is so important. Strong families make strong churches.

Chapter Thirteen

We Are Joyous People

Where is the joy the Lord Jesus promised? There is such a thing as the right side and the wrong side, but what about the bright side? I believe the Lord Jesus can put us on the bright side of life. He said, *"that my joy might remain in you, and that your joy might be full"* (John 15:11). I want that joy!

We Love One Another

Having true love for one another rids the church of gossip, backbiting, and busybodies. It rids the church of criticism. It rids the church of people who talk about someone's children when they happen to be going through a hard time. Everyone is going to have a hard time sooner or later. You are not much of a Christian and neither am I if we take advantage of someone's difficulties to criticize him, if we think we can be exalted by his failure and heartache. May God help us to be a church that loves one another.

We Are Deeply Committed to the Task of World Evangelism

We should be so committed to world evangelism that we study world geography for the purpose of knowing where people are, where churches are, and what people believe so we can get the gospel to those without Christ. We are committed to world evangelism. When we think of the world, we think of it this way.

We Take the High Road

Stay on the high road! The high road is not choosing between the good and the bad, but between the good and the best. Christ is the best and we are following after Christ. The high road is the unending pursuit of Jesus Christ.

We Place the Proper Emphasis on the Lord's Day

I know this is out of step with many churches today. I know that there are specific things that are of necessity and acts of mercy that need to be done on the Lord's Day; but I believe that a church should be exemplary in placing the proper emphasis on the Lord's Day.

Stay far away from organized sports on Sunday. The worst thing you can do for your family is substitute something for the worship of God.

We Are a Believing Church

These are things that should be clear about our church. I have said all of this to bring this emphasis. If we do all these things that I have mentioned to you and we are not people of faith, we will not accomplish what God wants us to accomplish. We must be a believing church, exercising faith in God.

The Membership of the Believing Church

I have a family. I have a wife, children, and grandchildren. As an individual, I must have faith in God; but my family also must have faith in God. As an individual, I have a testimony. As a family, we have a testimony. It should mean something to my family to bear the name that I have as a family name. There was a day when one's family name meant something to people. I am saying to you that in a believing church, we are a family.

Please understand what it means when you come to place your life and influence in a local New Testament church. The idea most people have today is to never really join a church, just to simply attend a church. This is not scriptural.

Chapter Thirteen

We need to be identified with a local assembly of believers. We need to call a church our church home. We need to say, "This is the place where we worship God. This is the church to which we belong. This is where we place our life and influence as members of this church."

You have a family. You have an identity. You identify with that family name. In our church, we should identify with our church and what our church believes and does. This is why it is important in the membership of the church that all of us understand that there are certain things that should characterize each member of a believing church.

> *We should live beyond the limitations placed on us by men and what they believe can be done. We must live beyond man-made goals and objectives.*

Again and again we find this emphasis in the first century church. The Bible says things like, *"they went to their own company"* (Acts 4:23). The Bible says that Paul *"assayed to join himself to the disciples"* (Acts 9:26). These expressions reveal to us the matter of belonging.

We are people of faith in the true and living God. Many years ago when I came to the church I presently pastor, I met with a certain group of men and we prayed together about my invitation to speak in view of a call to be the pastor of the church. I said to them on that particular occasion, "I want to be the pastor of a church that will believe God for the things God wants us to do in this world. I do not want to be the pastor of a church that wants to fight and grumble about things."

The first century church was a believing church. There are times when we pause. We stand still to wait on God. Some of that standing still is to wait on God's people, to give them time to pray and seek the face of God and to know this is the way the Lord wants us to go.

It is extremely important to understand what it means to be a member of a believing church. The testimony we have as a church family is that we attempt what God wants us to attempt and we trust God to bring it to pass.

I hope it means a great deal to you to be identified with a local assembly of believers that is unashamed to be a first century church. The things we find in the New Testament about purity, decency, and biblical order–let those same things always be our testimony, and may we always be people who believe God and attempt things for God.

The Motive of the Believing Church

What motivates us? It can never be buildings or crowds. It can never be attendance goals. It can never be big days or campaigns.

There is only one motive that will please God. All other motives must be judged by that one motive. It comes in the definition of faith–*"looking unto Jesus."* The motive for a believing church is obedience to the Lord Jesus Christ. Are we following after Him? Does it please Him? Is this what He wants?

There is a refining process going on in our lives on a daily basis. The things God uses to refine me are the same types of things God uses to refine you. There are certain things He spells out in Scripture. He uses necessities. He uses reproaches. He uses persecution. He uses distresses. He uses infirmities. He uses the same things He used in the lives of the apostles.

The Bible says in II Corinthians 12:1-10,

> *It is not expedient for me doubtless to glory. I will come to visions and revelations of the Lord. I knew a man in Christ above fourteen years ago, (whether*

> *in the body, I cannot tell; or whether out of the body, I cannot tell: God knoweth;) such an one caught up to the third heaven. And I knew such a man, (whether in the body, or out of the body, I cannot tell: God knoweth;) how that he was caught up into paradise, and heard unspeakable words, which it is not lawful for a man to utter. Of such an one will I glory: yet of myself I will not glory, but in mine infirmities. For though I would desire to glory, I shall not be a fool; for I will say the truth: but now I forbear, lest any man should think of me above that which he seeth me to be, or that he heareth of me. And lest I should be exalted above measure through the abundance of the revelations, there was given to me a thorn in the flesh, the messenger of Satan to buffet me, lest I should be exalted above measure. For this thing I besought the Lord thrice, that it might depart from me. And he said unto me, My grace is sufficient for thee: for my strength is made perfect in weakness. Most gladly therefore will I rather glory in my infirmities, that the power of Christ may rest upon me. Therefore I take pleasure in infirmities, in reproaches, in necessities, in persecutions, in distresses for Christ's sake: for when I am weak, then am I strong.*

God gives you an infirmity. God gives you a necessity, something you must deal with. God gives you persecution. God gives you distress. God gives you reproach. These are things God uses to deal with us. Why does He do it? Is it because He delights in bringing those things into our lives? No. It is because He is refining us so that our motive always remains the Person of Jesus Christ.

There is a strength that makes us weak, and there is a weakness that makes us strong. It is His strength we need and His strength is made perfect in our weakness.

By the way, this is not just for the ministry; it is for all our lives. If you are pursuing an education, why are you doing it? It should be to honor and bring glory to God. My wife and I have been married since 1967. The idea about marriage is that as a Christian, I can bring glory to God this way. She and I can serve the Lord together in a way that brings more glory to God. If something comes into our marriage that does not bring glory to God, that does not please the Lord, it needs to be dealt with and given to God.

Faith is *"looking unto Jesus."* In a believing church, the motive is always the Lord Jesus Christ.

THE METHODS OF THE BELIEVING CHURCH

As a believing church, we must also give consideration to our methods. This is one of the great pitfalls today. Many church leaders are doing nearly anything to get a crowd to attend.

What methods should we use? Constantly we hear, "The message must always remain the same, but the methods change." No, friend, the methods must not change. The means change.

Recently, I made a quick trip to the state of Florida, 725 miles away. I traveled there by means of an airplane. There are means available to be used today to accomplish things. There are computers and electronic devices, there are faster ways of printing–these are means. But the methods must always be biblical.

The believing church is not built on activity. Activity becomes a substitute for spirituality. After a while one cannot tell the difference between what people call a church and some sort of gathering to motivate people. Why? Because the whole idea becomes an ambitious venture, not an act of obedience to God. It is man-centered, not Christ-centered.

What is a believing church? A believing church is a church that has faith in God and attempts great things for God. A believing church is not a group sitting around saying, "We have faith in God." A believing church is launching out into the deep. It is pressing on, advancing for the Lord.

Make note of what the Bible says in James 2:14-20,

> *What doth it profit, my brethren, though a man say he hath faith, and have not works? can faith save him? If a brother or sister be naked, and destitute of daily food, and one of you say unto them, Depart in peace, be ye warmed and filled; notwithstanding ye give them not those things which are needful to the body; what doth it profit? Even so faith, if it hath not works, is dead, being alone. Yea, a man may say, Thou hast faith, and I have works: shew me thy faith without thy works, and I will shew thee my faith by my works. Thou believest that there is one God; thou doest well: the devils also believe, and tremble. But wilt thou know, O vain man, that faith without works is dead?*

What about this believing church? The believing church takes the gospel to the ends of the earth. The believing church goes into the highways and hedges. The believing church walks across the street to a neighbor. The believing church finds those who are hurting and tells them about God who can heal their hurting heart.

This believing church finds out how many streets and highways there are in their city and who lives on those streets and highways. They go up and down those streets and highways, door to door, telling people about Jesus Christ. The believing church prints gospel literature that clearly lifts up the Lord to give to everyone. This believing church gets into all the world with the gospel.

A believing church does not sit around and say, "We have faith." A believing church rises up and works harder than the crowd that simply puts up a billboard and waits for everyone to come. A believing church gets the seed out of the barn and sows it in the field.

A believing church is influential, and that influence is felt where people are. People in places of business notice that the members of that church are "different" in the right way. Co-workers and employers notice that the members come to work on time and work hard. A believing church demonstrates the right kind of life on a daily basis.

A believing church gives out gospel tracts and speaks to people about the Lord Jesus. A member of a believing church will get on an elevator in a local hospital and hand a gospel tract to someone. The person on the elevator may say, "I've got one of these already," because someone else from that believing church has already been there.

We need to understand that a believing church does not sit around the church house and talk about what they are going to do. A believing church rises up and gets the gospel out to people. This is what every town and community needs–a believing church. May God help us to be a believing church.

Dr. Peter Masters, pastor of the Metropolitan Tabernacle, shared with me an interesting story about Spurgeon's ministry, which exemplifies a believing church.

He explained that many had the idea when Spurgeon preached, people from all over London came out of the woodwork to hear the great Spurgeon; but it was not that way. There were many people in the church who took the message he preached into the highways and hedges every week and got the message out to the people where they lived and worked. They brought these people with them to hear their pastor. This was the secret.

The matter under consideration is a very simple one. The first century church took seriously what Christ said and moved forward in obedience to Him.

The great divide between them and what we find today is people who do not take seriously what He said and do not take action. To change the future, we must disturb the present. A real revolution back to the Bible will disturb the present and will change the future.

I leave you with this–it is a word from one of the powerful preachers of the first century. James declared, *"Therefore to him that knoweth to do good, and doeth it not, to him it is sin"* (James 4:17).